WINSTON CHUR
OXFORDSHIRE HUSSA

Edited by Stanley C. Jenkins

Design & Layout

ISBN 9781899889433
© Lightmoor Press and Stanley Jenkins, 2009

Contents

Introduction 1
Foreword 3
A Churchill Chronology 4
Birth & Early Years 7
Active Soldier 13
Polititian & Statesman 45
High Society 55
Operation 'Hope Not' – Winston's Funeral 61

INTRODUCTION

It would probably be no exaggeration to say that Sir Winston Churchill is one of the most famous people in history. His long and eventful life has been the subject of innumerable books and articles, and it is, at first glance, difficult to see what more could said about this great statesman and war leader. There are, however, one or two more or less neglected aspects of his life, notably the links that existed between Winston, the Churchill family and the Oxfordshire Yeomanry – The Queens Own Oxfordshire Hussars.

Winston's association with the Queens Own Oxfordshire Hussars lasted for a much longer period than has hitherto been assumed, while he was also far more active and deeply involved with this part-time cavalry regiment than has been supposed. He first appeared with the rank of captain as second-in-command of the Woodstock Squadron on 19th November 1901 – his rank and appointment reflecting past service with the regular army. Thereafter, Winston maintained a life-long interest in 'his' Yeomanry regiment, becoming its Hon. Colonel in 1951. On his death, fourteen years later, a contingent of the Queens Own Oxfordshire Hussars were the fifth detachment of soldiers in the funeral procession – in effect the place of honour just ahead of the coffin.

In 2008, it was suggested that the Oxfordshire Yeomanry Trust might mount a Winston Churchill exhibition at the Oxfordshire Museum, Woodstock, which would explore Winston's links with Oxfordshire, Woodstock and the Queens Own Oxfordshire Hussars. This 'special Churchill edition' of *Bugle & Sabre*, was designed to accompany the exhibition – although it is hoped that the resulting publication will also be of interest to those with an interest in military and local history.

The main sections are arranged in a generally chronological progression, starting with Winston's birth and early life, and ending with his death in 1965. The 'Military' and 'Political' sections continue this chronological sequence, although the 'High Society' section has a more thematic approach, insofar as Winston's links with the rich and famous continued throughout his life.

Stanley C. Jenkins, Witney, 2009

Cover: **A portrait by the Irish painter Sir John Lavery RA (1856-1941), showing Winston Churchill in the uniform of the Queens Own Oxfordshire Hussars during World War I. His French 'Adrian' helmet is decidedly non-standard equipment for a British officer!** *The National Portrait Gallery*

Bugle & Sabre Special

Winston at his desk, from a photograph dated 25th April 1925.

Hugh Bourn Collection

Bugle & Sabre Special

FOREWORD

Soldiers of Oxfordshire are proud to present the exhibition that accompanies this book.

In the extensive literature dealing with his life, Winston Churchill's biographers have paid scant attention to his long career in the Oxfordshire Hussars. Our Exhibition shows that, following his early career as a regular Cavalry officer and war correspondent, and his dramatic Boer War adventures, Churchill lost little time in joining the Queens Own Oxfordshire Hussars at the beginning of 1901. Posted to the Henley Squadron, he put his active service experience to good use.

He was given command at Henley in 1905 and retained it until forced to give up by the demands of national office at the outbreak of war in 1914. Our records show that, during his thirteen years with the QOOH, Churchill's cavalry expertise and leadership skills were not wasted. Despite the high social aspirations of his regiment, the role of the dilettante 'social' officer was not for him. Churchill proudly drove his Henley Squadron in 1911 to be selected as the most militarily proficient reserve Cavalry Squadron in the British Army - thereby earning the 'privilege' of ten days exercising on Salisbury Plain with the Household Cavalry in addition to the annual two week camp. To achieve this, Churchill persuaded his Volunteers to drill up to three times a week extra in order to acquire the proficiency needed to win the competition. He did this at the same time as occupying a number of great offices of State.

Churchill served briefly in the QOOH again after World War I, when the Regiment had assumed a role in the Royal Artillery, and in his last years he became Honorary Colonel. Churchill's Yeomanry service is manifest proof of his view that the enthusiastic amateur can make a significant contribution to success in war. In the Oxfordshire Hussars, and in all his subsequent career, Churchill liked the company of people who 'thought outside the box'. Indeed, he sometimes seemed to prefer to employ them rather than those with conventional ideas.

This exhibition is one of a series by presented by the Soldiers of Oxfordshire. They are part of the Soldiers of Oxfordshire Project which is, in partnership with Oxfordshire County Council Museum Service, well advanced in its progress towards a new Military Museum and Research Centre, which will be built in the grounds of the Oxfordshire Museum in Woodstock.

The Trustees wish to thank the many individuals and organisations that have so freely given their assistance and advice, and who have furnished many of the artefacts, documents and pictures on show. They are listed below. The Trustees also wish to recognise in particular the contributions made by Stanley Jenkins, the author of the text in this book, and by Harry Staff, an endlessly resourceful and enthusiastic Curator. Hugh Babington Smith, our Project Officer has also made a contribution well beyond the call of duty.

Tim May
Deputy Chairman, Soldiers of Oxfordshire Trust

ACKNOWLEDGEMENTS

The Lady Soames
Hugh Bourn
Allen Packwood, Churchill Archive
Dr Lynsey Robertson, Churchill Archive
James Joll, Churchill Archive
Minnie Churchill
Phil Read, The Churchill Exhibition, London
Sarah Lewery, Churchill Archive
The Churchill Centre, Washington
Winston Churchill
Yvonne Churchill
Christine Beresford
The Buckinghamshire Military Museum Trust
Heather Carter, Blenheim Palace
The Dulverton Trust
Gerald Flint-Shipman
John Forster, Blenheim Palace
Michael Fisk
Sir Jeremy Greenstock, The Ditchley Foundation
Brigadier Christopher Galloway, The Ditchley Foundation
Ron and Betty Hickman
Isis Publishing Ltd
The Duke of Marlborough
Commanding Officer, Oxford University Officers Training Corps
Owen Mumford Ltd
Oxfordshire County Council
Oxfordshire Yeomanry Trust
The Friends of the Oxfordshire and Buckinghamshire Light Infantry
Carol Anderson, The Oxfordshire Museum
Cherry Gray, The Oxfordshire Museum
Christiane Jeuckens, Museum Resources Centre
Karen Winfield, The Oxfordshire Museum
Judge Douglas Russell
Philippa Rawlinson, Chartwell National Trust
The Royal Green Jackets Museum Trust
Vicky Stubbs, Chartwell National Trust

— Bugle & Sabre Special —

A CHURCHILL CHRONOLOGY

1874	30th November – Born at Blenheim Palace, Woodstock, Oxfordshire, the elder son of Lord Randolph Churchill. (*see p.7*)
1877	January – Winston is taken to live with his parents in Dublin. (*p.9*)
1880	The Churchills leave Ireland and return to England. (*p.10*)
1882	November, seven year old Winston is sent away to St. George's School at Ascot. (*p.10*)
1888	Winston entered Harrow School. (*pp.10-11*)
1889	September 1889 – Winston enters the Army Class at Harrow. (*p.13*)
1893	Entered The Royal Military College, Sandhurst. (*p.13-14*)
1895	Gazetted to 4th Hussars. (*p.15*)
1895	October – Observed the Spanish army in action against rebel forces in Cuba. (*pp.15-16*)
1897	Attached to the 31st Punjab Infantry while serving with the Malakand Field Force on the North-West Frontier of India. (*pp.16-17*)
1898	Served as an orderly officer to Sir W. Lockhart with the Tirah Expeditionary Force. (*p.17*)
1898	Attached to the 21st Lancers while serving with the Nile Expeditionary Force, and present at the Battle of Omderman on 2nd September. (*pp.17-20*)
1899	Defeated as a Conservative candidate in a by-election at Oldham in Lancashire. (*p.20, 45*)
1899-1900	Served as a Lieutenant in the South African Light Horse and as a correspondent with the *Morning Post* newspaper. Taken prisoner by the Boers on 15th November 1899 but escaped on 12th December 1899. (*p.20-26*)
1900	Elected as one of two Conservative Members of Parliament for Oldham.
1901	Made his maiden speech in the House of Commons. (*p.45, 47*)
1901	Gazetted to the Queens Own Oxfordshire Hussars. (*pp.26-40, 45, 58, 59, 61*)
1904	31st May – Crossed the Floor of the House and joined the Liberal Party. (*pp.27, 46*)
1906-1908	Served as Liberal MP for North-West Manchester and Under Secretary of State for the Colonies. (*p.46*)
1907	Appointed as a Privy Councillor.
1908	12th September – Married Miss Clementine Hozier, the daughter of the Colonel Sir Henry Hozier and Lady Blanche Hozier. (*p.56*)
1908-1922	Served as Liberal MP for Dundee. (*p.48*)
1908-1910	President of the Board of Trade. (*p.48*)
1909	Birth of a daughter, Diana.
1910-1911	Served as Home Secretary in Herbert Asquith's Liberal government. (*p.48*)
1911	3rd January 1911 – Was present at the 'Sidney Street Siege' in east London. (*p.48*)
1911	Birth of his only son, Randolph Frederick Edward.
1911-1915	Served as First Lord of the Admiralty. (*pp.29, 37-42, 57*)
1913	Appointed an Elder Brother of Trinity House.
1914	Birth of a daughter, Sarah Millicent Hermione.
1914-1918	Lord Rector of Aberdeen University.

1915	Served as chancellor of the Duchy of Lancaster before resigning from office in order to return to active service in the army.
1916	Lieutenant-Colonel commanding the 6th Royal Scots Fusiliers on the Western Front. (*pp.42, 58*)
1917	Minister of Munitions.
1918	Birth of a daughter, Marigold Frances (who died in 1921).
1919-1921	Secretary of State for War and for Air.
1921	February-April – Secretary of State for Air and for the Colonies.
1921-1922	Secretary of State for the Colonies.
1922	Birth of a daughter, Mary.
1922	Appointed a Companion of Honour.
1922	Defeated (as Liberal) at General Election. (*p.48*)
1924	Elected as the 'Constitutionalist' MP for Epping, in Essex. (*p.48*)
1924	Joined the Conservative Party.
1924-1929	Served as the Chancellor of the Exchequer.
1929-1945	Served as Conservative MP for Epping.
1929-1932	Lord Rector of Edinburgh University.
1929	Chancellor of Bristol University.
1939-1940	First Lord of the Admiralty.
1940-1945	Prime Minister of Great Britain & Northern Ireland, First Lord of the Treasury and Minister of Defence. (*p.44, 49-53*)
1941	Appointed Lord Warden of the Cinque Ports.
1941	Elected a Fellow of the Royal Society.
1945	Served as Conservative MP for Woodford in Essex.
1945-1951	Leader of the Opposition.
1946	Appointed a member of the Order of Merit.
1948	Honorary Academician Extraordinary of the Royal Academy.
1951	Succeeded Queen Mary as Hon Colonel of the Queens Own Oxfordshire Hussars.
1951-1955	Prime Minister and First Lord of the Treasury.
1953	Created a Knight Companion of the Honourable and Noble Order of the Garter in St Georges Chapel at Windsor Castle.
1953	Awarded the Nobel Prize for Literature.
1959	One-man show at Royal Academy.
1963	Proclaimed an honorary citizen of the United States of America. (*p.61*)
1965	Suffered a stroke on 15th January and died on Sunday 24th January, interment at Bladon, near Woodstock, taking place on 30th January after a state funeral in St. Paul's Cathedral. The Queens Own Oxfordshire Hussars were chosen to lead the funeral cortège. (*pp.61, 64*)

A charcoal portrait sketch of Winston's mother, Lady Randolph Churchill (1854-1921) by the American painter John Singer Sargent (1856-1925). Lady Randolph was the daughter of Leonard Jerome of New York, and one of the most glamorous figures in Victorian and Edwardian society.
The National Portrait Gallery

BIRTH & EARLY YEARS

Winston's Birth

Winston Leonard Spencer Churchill was born, appropriately, in his ancestral home of Blenheim Palace, at Woodstock in Oxfordshire, on 30th November 1874. His father, Lord Randolph Churchill (1849-1895), was a brilliant politician, while his mother Jennie (1854-1921) was one of the most glamorous figures in Victorian society. Three days later, *The Times* announced: 'On 30th November at Blenheim Palace, the Lady Randolph Churchill, prematurely, of a son'. The baby was baptised in the chapel at Blenheim Palace on 27th December.

The name Winston Leonard Spencer Churchill was an amalgam of Winston's ancestry. The first Winston Churchill, the father of the great Duke of Marlborough, was a Dorset squire who had married a relative of Francis Drake and fought for the Royalists during the Civil War. Leonard was the name of Winston's maternal grandfather, Leonard Jerome (1817-91), a wealthy American who owned *The New York Times* and had founded the first great racecourses in America – the Jerome Park course and the Coney Island Jockey Club.

The Setting

Woodstock, Winston's birthplace, is a small, Cotswold stone town, situated some six miles to the north-west of Oxford. In ancient times, this area of Oxfordshire was part of the Forest of Wychwood, and many of the surrounding villages have Saxon names relating to trees or woodland. The Domesday Book records that Woodstock was a Royal Manor, and in medieval times the Plantagenet kings frequently stayed in the area. Henry I built a hunting lodge here in the early 12th century, enclosing part of Wychwood Forest to form a 'Park', while Henry's grandson Henry II also spent much of his time at Woodstock, enlarging the hunting lodge and granting 'divers portions of … the demesne … to divers men for the purpose of building lodgings therein'.

Woodstock remained a Royal Palace throughout the Middle Ages. Henry III escaped assassination there in 1238, while Edward III and Queen Philippa resided in the medieval palace on several occasions, notably in 1330 when the Queen gave birth to Edward, the Black Prince – the hero of Crécy. Woodstock was in decline during the

An Edwardian postcard view of Blenheim Palace, looking west towards the main block, with the Kitchen Court and orangery visible to the right. It is believed that this card was posted by a newly-appointed chamber maid. *Stanley C. Jenkins Collection*

Tudor period - though its royal associations continued when the future Elizabeth I was imprisoned in the old palace by her half-sister, the Catholic Mary I. In 1642 the decaying (and probably half-ruinous) medieval palace was garrisoned by Royalist forces as part of an outer rim of defences protecting the King's headquarters at Oxford.

The town was surrendered to Parliament on 26th April 1646 and what was left of the royal palace was demolished in 1651, although Woodstock remained a royal manor until 1704, in which year the property was conferred on John Churchill, the First Duke of Marlborough, as a reward for his great victory over Louis IV at the Battle of Blenheim.

Although Winston spent the first few years of his life in Ireland and was then sent away to boarding school, he was a frequent visitor to Blenheim, which he clearly regarded as his ancestral home. As late as the 1960s, he was remembered locally as a precocious, red-headed child; one day he was out riding, and rather than say 'excuse me' to a village girl who had innocently blocked his path, he threatened to get down from his horse and whip her out of the way. 'If you do that', she answered, 'I'll tan your hide, and what is more I'll tell your grandma'; understandably alarmed at this mention of his formidable grandmother (the Seventh Duchess), young Winston trotted back to the palace. Other stories recall the future Prime Minister hitching lifts to Hanborough station on the back of farm wagons and carriers' carts, and sitting on the back with his feet dangling over the tailboard!

Winston's Illustrious Ancestor

John Churchill, Winston's most famous ancestor, was, in the opinion of Sir Charles Oman, 'by far the greatest military man that England had ever known'. As a soldier he was the founder of 'a new school of scientific strategy; on the battle-field he was alert and vigorous, but he was greater in the operations that precede a battle'. When Britain embarked upon The War of the Spanish Succession against Louis XIV of France, Marlborough was chosen to command the forces sent to Europe to join the Austrians and Dutch. Marlborough's first great campaign was that of 1704. When it opened, the French and their Bavarian allies were planning to attack Vienna, but Marlborough countered this threat by a rapid advance across Germany, after first carrying out a series of skilful feints which led the French to believe that he was about to invade Alsace.

Having thoroughly misled the French he appeared m the valley of the Danube, and by storming the fortified camp of the Bavarians he placed his army between the enemy and Austria, and thereby prevented any further advance towards Vienna. When joined by an Austrian army under Prince Eugene of Savoy, Marlborough was strong enough to defeat the whole force of the French and Bavarians at a marshy stream called the Nebel, which falls into the Danube near the village of Blenheim. 'Eleven thousand men laid down their arms in Blenheim village when they saw that their retreat was cut off; 15,000 more were drowned, slain, or wounded, and not half the Franco-Bavarian army succeeded in escaping'. This crushing blow saved Austria and humbled the over-mighty Louis XIV. The whole of Bavaria fell into Marlborough's hands, the French retired behind the Rhine and Germany was saved from further French attacks.

A grateful nation rewarded Marlborough by giving him the royal manor of Woodstock, a sum of £500,000 being granted by Parliament to build a baroque palace that would rival anything in Europe. Designed by Sir John Vanbrugh and Nicholas Hawksmoor, Blenheim Palace was built near the site of Henry II's old hunting lodge and eventually cost around £300,000, much of this sum having been provided by the Duchess of Marlborough because only half of the money voted by Parliament was ever paid.

The palace took over twenty years to build and it eventually covered seven acres – at one time over 1,500 workmen were employed in its construction. This massive structure was replete with military symbolism, its external ornamentation being composed chiefly of spears, flags and cannon balls, while the rectangular plan of the main block, with its four massive towers, resembled that of a fortress. When finally completed in 1725, this magnificent palace was not unlike Versailles – that symbol of an over-mighty French monarch, whose ambitions had been humbled on the field of Blenheim on 13th August 1704.

Lord Randolph Churchill & The Fourth Party

In 1883 the Blenheim estate passed to George Charles Spencer Churchill (1844-1892), the Eighth Duke of Marlborough. Although the new Duke had inherited the estate and title, he was in many ways overshadowed by his younger brother, the dashing Lord Randolph Churchill. In 1874, Lord Randolph - then only twenty-five – had been elected Conservative Member of Parliament for Woodstock, and this ambitious young politician spent much time at Blenheim.

By the 1880s, Lord Randolph had emerged as leader of the so-called 'Fourth Party' – an unofficial grouping of younger Tories who hoped to present their political creed to the masses in a popular and exciting way. Like other third or fourth parties, it was sometimes difficult to see what the Fourth Party stood for, but there was no doubting its grass roots popularity. Huge rallies became a feature of political life, and Lord Randolph, together with his striking American wife Jennie would tour the great centres of population in a conscious and unashamed attempt to 'woo the masses'.

The Primrose League

Politics were at that time in a state of flux. The Franchise Bill of 1884 had increased the size of the British electorate from 3,000,000 to 5,000,000 and, at a time when Gladstone's Liberal Party was seen as a party of free-trading, *laisser-faire* industrialists, the Tories began to portray themselves as champions of the working man, as well as a party of great landowners. To further this aim, a group of Fourth Party MPs founded an organisation known as the Primrose League - a political society which was supposed to 'embrace all classes and all creeds except atheists and enemies of the British Empire'. Lady Randolph rapidly became a leading figure in this new organisation, while the Duchess of Marlborough was made President of the Ladies' Grand Council.

The Fourth Party and the Primrose League were both intimately connected with Blenheim, and, although the borough of Woodstock was disfranchised in 1885, Lord Randolph – a superb orator with an instinctive understanding of the masses – must have realised that his ancestral home would provide a splendid, theatrical setting for speeches and political rallies. However, as Lady Randolph later recalled, 'the distances to cover were great, and motors were not in existence'. To obviate this problem the Marlboroughs formed an undertaking known as The Woodstock Railway Company with the aim of constructing a rail link to Woodstock. This worthy project was brought to a successful conclusion on Monday 19th May 1890, when the railway was opened from Kidlington to a new station at 'Blenheim & Woodstock'.

Winston's Colourful Ancestry

Winston's ancestry was exceedingly colourful, his mother's family, the Jeromes, being descended from Huguenots who had sailed to America from the Isle of Wight in 1710, while Lady Randolph was also said to have had native American blood – one of her ancestors being Meribah, an Iroquois woman who had married an English settler in Massachusetts. On his father's side, Winston had a distinct Irish connection, his paternal grandmother being Francis Vane Tempest, Countess of Antrim, a descendant of the MacDonnells of Antrim.

Winston's Early Childhood

Winston's Irish heritage is often overlooked although, when he was barely a year old, his grandfather the Seventh Duke of Marlborough was appointed to the post of Viceroy of Ireland, and Lord Randolph became his private secretary. The Marlboroughs travelled to Ireland in January 1877 and, for the next three years, Winston's home was the 'The Little Lodge', within the grounds of the Vice-Regal Lodge at Dublin. Winston's earliest memories were thus of Ireland, rather than England – one of the events which remained firmly in his memory being a minor accident when he fell from a donkey which had been frightened by a group of men whom his nurse, Mrs Everest, claimed were 'Fenians' – though it is perhaps more likely that they were British soldiers!

Winston also remembered his mother Jennie who, during his Irish childhood, was often on horseback: *"She and my father hunted continually on their large horses; and sometimes there were great scares because one or the other did not come back for many hours after they were expected. My mother always seemed to me a fairy princess: a radiant being possessed of limitless riches and power. She shone for me like the evening Star. I loved her dearly – but at a distance"*.

A letter written by Winston to his mother, thanking her for the gift of some toy soldiers. Winston had a large collection of toy soldiers, which were laid-out on a baseboard, complete with forts and other accessories. *The Chartwell Trust*

The Churchills returned to England early in 1880, shortly after the birth of Winston's younger brother John Strange Spencer Churchill (1880-1947), who was known among friends and family as 'Jack'.

Mrs Everest

As a member of the Victorian aristocracy Winston had a lonely childhood, his parents being aloof and distant figures who lived very full lives that left little time for intimate contact with their children. Under these circumstances Winston was brought up by his devoted 'nanny', Mrs Elizabeth Everest (1833-1895), who became a surrogate parent and was able to provide the love and attention that would otherwise have been lacking.

Mrs Everest had gone into service with the Churchills in 1875, a few months after Winston's birth, and she remained with the family until 1893. She had been born in Chatham but, as far as can be ascertained, she never married – 'Mrs' being an honorary title. Winston, who called her 'Woom', or 'Woomany', wrote in his autobiography: *"My nurse was my confidante. Mrs Everest it was who looked after me and tended all my wants. It was to her I poured out all my many troubles. Before she came to us, she had brought up for twelve years a little girl called Ella, the daughter of a clergyman who lived in Cumberland"*.

When Mrs Everest died of peritonitis at her sister's house in North London on 3rd July 1895, Winston, who had rushed to her bedside, immediately sent a telegram to the clergyman, the Venerable Thompson Phillips, and they met at the funeral in Manor Park Cemetery, East London. In a letter to his mother, Winston said that *"all her relatives were there – a good many of whom had travelled from Ventnor overnight – and I'm quite surprised to find how many friends she had made in her quiet and simple life. The coffin was covered with wreaths and everything was as it should be"*.

Winston paid for 'Woomany's' headstone, and his son Randolph recalled that 'For many years afterwards he paid an annual sum to the local florist for the upkeep of the grave'. It is thought that Mrs Everest was the inspiration for the hero's housekeeper, Bettine, who features in Winston's novel *Savrola* (1900).

Winston's Unhappy Schooldays

In November 1882, at the age of seven, Winston was sent away to St. George's School at Ascot. Its headmaster was the Reverend H. W. Sneyd-Kynnersley – an Anglican clergyman who indulged in periodic bouts of brutal thrashing. Winston's pugnacious and rebellious nature ensured that he received his full share of these canings, but they did not break his spirit. On one occasion he was beaten for stealing sugar from the pantry, and in revenge he kicked the headmaster's hat to pieces. In his memoir, *My Early Life* (1930), Winston recalled:

"The school my parents had selected for my education was one of the most fashionable and expensive in the country. It modelled itself upon Eton and aimed at being preparatory for that Public School above all others. It was supposed to be the very last thing in schools. Only ten boys in a class; electric light (then a wonder); a swimming pond; spacious football and cricket grounds; two or three school treats, or 'expeditions' as they were called, every term; the masters all MAs in gowns and mortar-boards; a chapel of its own; no hampers allowed; everything provided by the authorities.

It was a dark November afternoon when we arrived at this establishment. .... I was taken into a Form Room and told to sit at a desk. All the other boys were out of doors, and I was alone with the Form Master. He produced a thin greeny-brown, covered book filled with words in different types of print. 'You have never done any Latin before, have you?' he said. 'No sir' .... 'You must learn this', he said, pointing to a number of words in a frame of lines. 'I will come back in half an hour and see what you know. Behold me then on a gloomy evening, with an aching heart, seated in front of the First Declension. What on earth did it mean? Where was the sense of it? It seemed absolute rigmarole to me".

Winston never settled at Ascot and, after a year he became seriously ill and at the end of the 1884 summer term he was taken away. His next school, which was at 29 & 30 Brunswick Road, Hove, near Brighton, was a much gentler establishment run by two elderly maiden ladies. Miss Eva Moore, the actress, was the dancing mistress, and she considered that Winston was 'the naughtiest boy in the class. I used to think him the naughtiest small boy in the world!' In later years, Winston remembered that:

"This was a smaller school than the one I had left. It was also cheaper and less pretentious. But there was an element of kindness and of sympathy which I had found conspicuously lacking in my first experiences. At this school I was allowed to learn things which interested me: French, History, lots of Poetry by heart, and above all riding and swimming. The impression of those years makes a pleasant picture in my mind, in strong contrast to my earlier schoolday memories".

Despite the bracing seaside air of Brighton, Winston's chest remained very weak and indeed, on one occasion he nearly died of pneumonia. This presented an obvious dilemma for Lord Randolph, who had anticipated that his son would go to Eton College, among the damp meadows of the Thames Valley, where six generations of Churchills had been educated. At length, it was decided that Winston would be sent to Harrow, which was considered to have a much healthier location. In this context, it may be significant that Edward Marjoribanks (1849-1909), Lord Randolph's brother-in-law, had already decided to send his son to Harrow, and one assumes that discussions had taken place within the family.

How he got in remains something of a mystery, as a knowledge of Latin was an entry requirement for the school – yet Winston admitted that, when taking the entrance examination, his Latin paper consisted of *"the figure one, in brackets, a blot and some smudges"*. In the event the Headmaster, the Reverend James Edward Cowell Weldon (1854-1937), who had told Lord Randolph that he would find a place for Winston, admitted him in a mixture *"of faith and hope, not unmixed with charity"*.

Winston at Harrow

Much has been written about Winston's difficulties and apparent 'backwardness' at school, though it may be that the future Prime Minister was too much of an individualist to have done well at a Victorian public school. In subjects that he liked, such as History and English, he showed real ability, but in areas of study that he disliked, such as classics and mathematics, he made no effort whatsoever. At a time in which the ethos of public schools was dominated by the worship of rugby and cricket, young Winston made no secret of the fact that he disliked all team games, apart from polo, but he excelled at the supremely individualist sport of fencing – so much so that he won the Public Schools Fencing Championship.

He was also very keen on riding and swimming, and on one occasion he pushed a smaller boy into the swimming bath – his victim being the diminutive Leo Amery, one of the school's intellectual and athletic giants. Matters were not improved by Winston's attempted apology, when he said *"You were so small I thought you were a Fourth Form boy"*. However, in an attempt to make amends, he then added: *"My father, who is a great man, is also small!"*

Winston's other great interest at Harrow was the School Rifle Corps. A few days after he arrived at Harrow, on 3rd May 1888, the school magazine had printed an indignant letter from a correspondent who complained about the state of the Volunteer Rifle Corps. He said that the Corps should have at least 200 members, but it could muster barely half that number, and most of those were lazy and inefficient. The correspondent went on to consider the reason for this 'lack of energy and interest' in the Corps, which he attributed 'mainly to the fellows who belong to it themselves. The majority of them join merely for the pleasure of going to Wimbledon, and think it monstrous if they are obliged to attend twenty drills in the summer term. The consequence is that whenever the Corps makes its appearance the drilling is bad, the marching is slovenly, and it becomes the laughing stock of the rest of the School. That is why it is so difficult to get smart and influential fellows to join'. Winston, however, immediately joined the Volunteer Rifle Corps, and he appears to have regarded it as one of the more worthwhile aspects of his schooldays at Harrow.

Winston, who had plenty of brains when he chose to use them, also had a magnificent memory, and in his first term at Harrow he won a prize by repeating twelve hundred lines of Macaulay's *Lays of Ancient Rome* – the unashamed patriotism of these stirring verses being something which remained with him for the rest of his life. In his autobiography, written many years later, Winston made known his own views on education, which clearly reflected his own unhappy schooldays – *"I would make boys all learn English; and then I would let the clever ones learn Latin as an honour and Greek as a treat. But the only thing I would whip them for is not knowing English, I would whip them hard for that"*.

The Harrow School Songs

The Harrow School Songs also stirred his youthful patriotism. Churchill's son Randolph recalled that, in 1940, he had accompanied his father to an annual singing of the School Songs at Harrow. Driving back he said, emotionally:

"Listening to those boys singing all those well-remembered songs I could see myself fifty years before singing with them those tales of great deeds and of great men and wondering with intensity how I could ever do something glorious for my country".

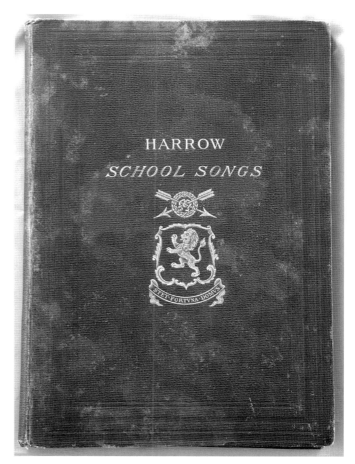

A copy of the Harrow School Songs book.
Hugh Bourn Collection

A photograph of Winston in QOOH uniform, taken possibly in a London square between 1905 and 1909. It is interesting to note that although this is obviously a formal occasion, Winston does not appear to be wearing a Queens Own Oxfordshire Hussars field Officers full dress jacket – after at least four years with the QOOH he fails to dress like his colleagues!.

Oxfordshire Yeomanry Trust OXYT584

ACTIVE SOLDIER

Winston's Toy Soldiers

Winston had a life-long interest in history, wars and the army – these subjects being, in his lively mind, merely the separate strands of one great historical tapestry. Woodstock Palace and its association with knighthood, chivalry and the Black Prince, was clearly one of his sources of inspiration, while Blenheim and the martial exploits of his ancestor the First Duke of Marlborough were even greater influences. When at home, his favourite amusement was playing with toy soldiers, of which he had an immense army, powerfully equipped with cavalry, limbers and cannon. John, his younger brother, was sometimes allowed to participate in Winston's complex war games, albeit as the commander of the native troops who, devoid of artillery and modern weapons, had to accept inevitable defeat when confronted by the massed ranks of Winston's imperial forces!

The Army Class at Harrow

Winston's army of toy soldiers featured in his choice of career. One day his father happened to see Winston playing with his miniature army – which was deployed on a wooden baseboard. Lord Randolph decided 'to inspect the troops' and, after spending about twenty minutes studying their competent dispositions he asked his scholastically 'backward' son if he would like to go into the Army? The reply being positive Winston's career was decided, and in September 1889 he entered the Army Class at Harrow.

The Army Class had been introduced by the Revered Welldon as part of his far-reaching reforms of the school curriculum. Although members of the Army Class remained nominal members of their regular forms, they were taken away from the main stream of ordinary school lessons and given special instruction in subjects which would help them to pass the entrance examinations for The Military Academy at Woolwich or the Royal Military College, Sandhurst. Not only did this involve extra lessons in the evenings and on half-holidays, but it also meant that it was difficult for Army Class boys to rise high enough in their ordinary forms to obtain a 'Remove' at the end of the term. In Winston's case, this meant that he never got out of The Lower School throughout his four and a half years at Harrow – although after three years he was no longer compelled to 'fag' for older boys.

In the event, Winston's subsequent performance in the Army class was disappointing. Mr Wellsford and Mr L.M.Moriarty, the Army Class tutors, did not think that his mathematical abilities were good enough for him to pass into the Military Academy at Woolwich, which prepared cadets for careers in the Royal Artillery or the Royal Engineers. It was therefore decided that Winston should try for a place at Sandhurst, which was geared primarily towards those seeking careers in the infantry or the cavalry.

Winston at Sandhurst

Having failed at his first attempt to pass the entrance examination for Sandhurst, Winston was entered for a second attempt, and on this occasion he came 203rd out of 664 candidates with a score of 6,106 marks – which was still not sufficient to secure a place at the Royal Military College. Following this second disappointment, he was sent to an army coaching establishment run by Captain Walter James, who managed to cram enough information into his head in order to get him through the examinations – albeit with a score that was too low to gain admittance as an infantry candidate. Winston was therefore sent to Sandhurst to be trained as a cavalry officer.

Cavalry commissions were less sought after than those in the infantry as they involved much heavier expenses, and Lord Randolph was keenly disappointed – not least because he would have to buy Winston a horse! Winston, who liked riding and swordsmanship, was nevertheless jubilant, and on 6th August 1893 he wrote a cheerful letter to his father, telling him of his success in passing the Sandhurst Entrance Examination. Lord Randolph's reply, dated 9th August 1893, was unbelievably cruel:

"My dear Winston,
I am rather surprised at your tone of exultation over your inclusion in the Sandhurst list. There are two ways of winning an examination, one creditable the other the reverse. You have unfortunately chosen the latter method, and appear to be much pleased with your success.

The first extremely discreditable feature of your performance was missing the infantry, for in that failure is demonstrated beyond refutation your slovenly happy-go-lucky harum scarum style of work for which you have always been distinguished at your different schools. Never have I received a really good report of your conduct in your work from any master or tutor you had from time to time to do with. Always behind-hand, never advancing in your class, incessant complaints of total want of application, and this character which was constant in your reports has shown the natural results clearly in your last army examination.

The second discreditable fact in the result of your examination is that you have not perceptibly increased as far as my memory serves me the marks you made in the examination, and perhaps even you have decreased them, in spite of there being less competition in the last than in the former examination. You frequently told me you were sure to obtain 7,000 marks. Alas! your estimate of your capacity was, measured arithmetically, some seven hundred marks deficient. You say in your letter there were many candidates who succeeded whom you knew;

I must remind you that you had very few below you some seven or eight. You may find some consolation in the fact that you have failed to get into the 60th Rifles one of the finest regiments in the army. There is also another satisfaction for you that by accomplishing the prodigious effort of getting into the Cavalry, you imposed on me an extra charge of some £200 a year. Not that I shall allow you to remain in the Cavalry. As soon as possible I shall arrange your exchange into an infantry regiment of the line.

Now it is a good thing to put this business very plainly before you. Do not think I am going to take the trouble of writing to you long letters after every folly and failure you commit and undergo. I shall not write again on these matters and you need not trouble to write any answer to this part of my letter, because I no longer attach the slightest weight to anything you may say about your own acquirements and exploits. Make this position indelibly impressed on your mind, that if your conduct and action at Sandhurst is similar to what it has been in the other establishments in which it has sought vainly to impart to you some education. Then that my responsibility for you is over."

Having threatened to break off all contact with his son, he ended with the stark warning:

"I am certain that if you cannot prevent yourself from leading the idle useless unprofitable life you have had during your schooldays and later months, you will become a mere social wastrel, one of the hundreds of the public school failures, and you will degenerate into a shabby, unhappy and futile existence. If that is so you will have to bear all the blame for such misfortunes yourself".

In 1893 Winston entered the Royal Military College. Although he was never a great scholar, his brilliant mind could readily master any subject for which he could see a use, and in this respect his Sandhurst days were remarkably successful: 'It was as if the early morning mists had suddenly cleared and the sun was now shining radiantly in a cloudless sky. He was no longer regarded as a dunce, but an able and successful embryo officer'. Winston finished his Sandhurst course in December 1894, his examination results being good enough to ensure that he came 20th out of 130 candidates (although in his autobiography Winston claimed to have been ranked 8th out of 150).

Improved Relations with Lord Randolph

Winston's success at Sandhurst seemed, at long last, to please his father, and at length Lord Randolph gradually began to show more understanding of Winston's interests and ambitions. In *My Early Life*, Winston gave a sympathetic account of his relations with his father at this time. In addition to trips to the races, or to the theatre, Lord Randolph also introduced Winston to some of his colleagues in the Conservative Party, which may have kindled an interest in politics, and the great issues of the day:

"Once I became a gentleman cadet I acquired a new status in my father's eyes. I was entitled when on leave to go about with him, if it was not inconvenient. He was always amused by acrobats, jugglers, and performing animals, and it was with him that I first visited the Empire Theatre.

He took me also to important political parties at Lord Rothschild's house at Tring, where most of the leaders and a selection of the rising men of the Conservative Party were often assembled. He began to take me also to stay with his racing friends; and here we had a different company and new topics of conversation which proved equally entertaining. In fact to me he seemed to own the key to everything or almost everything worth having. But if ever I began to show the slightest idea of comradeship, he was immediately offended; and when once I suggested that I might help his private secretary to write some of his letters, he froze me into stone. I know now that this would have been only a passing phase.

Had he lived another four or five years, he could not have done without me. But there were no four or five years! Just as friendly relations were ripening into an entente, and an alliance or at least a military agreement seemed to my mind not beyond the bounds of reasonable behaviour, he vanished for ever".

Lord Randolph's Illness

In November 1894, Winston was warned that his father was ailing, and near to death. The victim of an unfortunate illness, Lord Randolph's behaviour had become increasingly erratic and, having quarrelled with most of his colleagues, he had resigned from public office in 1887 (although he remained a Member of Parliament until his death). His career in ruins, this brilliant politician deteriorated slowly throughout the early 1890s and, as paralysis approached, he suffered from facial twitches, slurred speech and terrifying delusions.

In June 1894 Lord Randolph was sent on a world cruise – though he was by that time virtually insane, the affliction having reached his brain. In *My Early Life*, Winston remembered, poignantly, that in one of his last remarks, Randolph had asked 'have you got your horses?'

The true nature and severity of the illness had been kept more or less secret but, as Winston began to suspect the truth, he wrote to Dr Robson Roose (1848-1905), the family physician, and subsequent letters to his mother suggest that he had in fact seen his father's medical reports. On 8th November 1894, for example, Winston wrote the following letter to his mother from Sandhurst:

"My dearest darling Mamma,
I got yesterday a report of Papa from Yokohama. Dr Roose was good enough to let me see it. It describes his having been ill with numbness in the hand – I have no doubt you remember the occasion. I am very very sorry to hear that so little improvement has been made, and that apparently there is not much chance of improvement.

My darling Mummy - you must not be cross with me for

having persuaded Roose to keep me informed as I shall never tell anyone and it is only right I should know. Above all things you must not write to him and scold him - as I promised I would not tell anyone but have made an exception in your case. I hope and trust as sincerely as it is possible there may still be time for some improvement & some really favourable signs. Do please write and tell me all about him - quite unreservedly. You know you told me to write to you on every subject freely.
With best love my darling Mummy,
Ever your loving son WINSTON"

It is likely that, in all his life, Winston had only three or four really frank and intimate talks with his father - the failure to gain his confidence and friendship being particularly tragic in that Lord Randolph was a brilliant and lovable figure. Friends, colleagues and members of the general public adored him, while at the very end, when he rose in the Commons to attempt a speech and lost the thread of his argument, 'his fellow-members, friends and opponents alike, sat listening to the stricken man with no feeling but of sympathy and affection'. Lord Rosebery wrote that 'There was no curtain, no retirement, he died by inches in public'.

Lord Randolph's Death
Lord Randolph Churchill died in London on Thursday 24th January 1895, and on the following Monday his body was brought back to Woodstock by train for burial in nearby Bladon church yard. Huge multitudes lined the streets of London to watch his funeral cortège pass. In the course of a very full and entirely sympathetic obituary *The Oxfordshire Weekly News* reported his final journey as follows:

"The remains of the late Lord Randolph Churchill were on Monday removed from Grosvenor Square to Paddington Station for conveyance to Bladon Church, near Woodstock, where the interment took place … At Paddington the large crowd which had gathered had to be regulated by a force of police and the departure platform was kept private except to the friends. The large bridges spanning the station, and other platforms were densely packed with persons anxious to catch a sight of the coffin. The special train conveying the coffin and mourners to Woodstock left the station at 10 o'clock, all persons present respectfully uncovering. At Twyford, Goring and other intermediate stations small groups made a similar display of feeling. At Oxford there was a brief stoppage and the Bishop (Dr Stubbs) and his chaplain (Dr Yule) joined the train.

Woodstock was reached a few minutes before twelve. Upon the platform and at the entrance were the Mayor (Mr W. P. Clarke) and members of the Corporation with craped mace, and the Woodstock & Blenheim Fire Brigades, the local AOF of which Lord Randolph was formerly an honorary member; the Blenheim estate tenantry, and the Conservative Association. Large numbers of townspeople thronged the approaches, mourning being everywhere observable. The principal places of business were closed, and blinds were generally drawn at private residences. Within Woodstock Church, where the first part of the burial service was impressively rendered, there was a large congregation".

A few days after his father's funeral, Winston took steps to start his career and, his mother having sent a telegram to Colonel John Palmer Brabazon (1843-1922) and a letter to the Duke of Cambridge, Winston was gazetted as a cavalry officer in the 4th Hussars. He received his commission on 20th February, 1895, his pay being £120 per annum.

Sadly, Mrs Everest died a few months after Lord Randolph, and having suffered two bereavements in a short space of time, Winston became much closer to his widowed mother. He was, moreover, at the age of twenty, now the family breadwinner, as Lady Randolph's private income was rapidly dissipated or mortgaged. It was, perhaps, for this reason, that Winston decided to supplement his meagre income by becoming a journalist.

Winston in Cuba
In October 1895 Winston and his friend Reginald Barnes (1871-1946), a fellow officer in the 4th Hussars, obtained permission from their commanding officer, Colonel Brabazon, to visit Cuba, which was at that time in a state of insurrection against Spanish rule. At the same time, he arranged a contract with *The Daily Graphic* whereby he would be paid the not inconsiderable sum of £5 for every descriptive letter sent from the front. Strings were also pulled with the Spanish authorities, with the result that Winston was able to accompany a government column on an expedition into rebel-held territory – in modern parlance, he became an 'embedded' journalist with the Spanish army.

On 29th November 1895 the Spanish learned that 4,000 rebels under Maximo Gormez were camped a few miles to the east of Iguara and at 5.00 am on 30th November General Valdez set out from Arroyo Blanco in pursuit of the insurgents. Winston later wrote:

"There was a low mist as we moved off in the early morning, and all of a sudden the rear of the column was involved in firing. In those days when people got quite close together in order to fight, and used — partly at any rate — large-bore rifles to fight with, loud bangs were heard and smoke puffs or even flashes could be seen. The firing seemed about a furlong away and sounded very noisy and startling. As, however, no bullets seemed to come near me, I was easily reassured. I felt like the optimist who did not mind what happened, so long as it did not happen to him".

As Winston recalled in his book *My Early Life*, he had come under fire on his twenty-first birthday: *"for the first time I heard shots fired in anger and heard bullets strike flesh or whistle through the air"*. From that time onwards the column was in contact with the insurgents almost continually for the next three days. On the night of 1st December a bullet came through the hut in which Winston was sleeping, while another wounded an orderly just outside. Winston, who believed, from an early age, that he was destined for future greatness, seemed to have no fear of death in these minor engagements. On the following day he witnessed the attack by General Valdez in what came to be known as the battle of La Reforma:

"We advanced right across open ground under a very heavy fire. The General, a very brave man - in a white and gold uniform on a grey horse - drew a great deal of fire on to us and I heard enough bullets whistle and hum past to satisfy me for some time to come. He rode right up to within 500 yards of the enemy and there we waited till the fire of the Spanish infantry drove them from the position.

We had great luck in not losing more than we did - but as a rule the rebels shot very high. We stayed by the General all the time and so were in the most dangerous place in the field. The General recommended us for the Red Cross - a Spanish Decoration given to officers – and coming in the train yesterday, by chance I found Marshal Campos and his staff, who told me that it would be sent us in due course".

Winston's adventures in Cuba were a source of controversy in that many of the Liberals and radicals back in England supported the rebel cause, and complained that he should not have been involved with the Spanish forces. Other critics considered that, as a guest of the Spanish, he should not have written disparaging remarks about the efficiency of their army. Nevertheless, his Cuban experiences had enabled Winston to see shots fired in anger for the first time - and given him a lifelong penchant for afternoon siestas and Cuban cigars.

Winston Meets Bourke Cockran

The Cuban expedition also gave Winston an opportunity to visit New York, were he met the influential, Sligo-born lawyer William Bourke Cockran (1854-1923), who had emigrated from Ireland to America in 1871 and subsequently become the Democratic Member of Congress for New York. The flamboyant Irish-American politician made a great impression on Winston who, in a letter to his mother, described him as *"one of the most charming hosts and interesting men I have ever met"*.

In his book, *Thoughts and Adventures* (1932), Churchill later wrote of Cockran: *"I must record the strong impression which this remarkable man made upon my untutored mind. I have never seen his like, or in some respects his equal. With his enormous head, gleaming eyes and flexible countenance, he looked uncommonly like the portraits of Charles James Fox. It was not my fortune to hear any of his orations, but his conversation, in point, in pith, in rotundity in antithesis and in comprehension, exceeded anything I have ever heard"*. Contact with such men may have awakened in Winston's mind the idea that, after a year or two in the army, he might emulate his father and enter into politics.

Action on The North-West Frontier

On 11th September 1896, Winston sailed for India with his regiment aboard the 6,525 ton P & O liner *SS Britannia* – his arrival in the sub-continent being marred by an accident at Bombay in which he dislocated his shoulder while attempting to leap ashore from a small boat. A few months later, in the summer of 1897, Major-General Sir Binden Blood (1842-1940) led a punitive expeditionary force to the North-West Frontier to suppress the Afridis and other rebel tribesmen who, stirred-up by their mullahs, had attacked British outposts and looted friendly villages.

Winston was on leave in England when he heard of the insurgency, but he was so eager to see action that he rushed back to India, booking a passage on the *SS Rome*. As there was no room for him on Sir Binden's staff, he obtained a contract with *The Allahabad Pioneer* – the same paper which had published Rudyard Kipling's early writing – to justify his presence at Sir Binden Blood's headquarters. At the same time, after relentless 'pulling of strings', Lady Randolph arranged a similar contract with *The Daily Telegraph*, and thus, in September 1897, Winston joined a mixed Anglo-Indian force as it set out for the 'badlands' on the borders of India and Afghanistan, where the mullahs had declared a 'Jihad' against the infidels.

Winston & 'The Little Englanders'

Although Winston had travelled widely prior to his arrival in India, he had not, hitherto, experienced the sheer scale of the British Empire. His arrival in the sub-continent was, therefore, a source of inspiration for the aspiring politician. Winston was already an unashamed imperialist who despised the small-minded 'Little Englanders' who were starting to become predominant in radical circles. Something of his pro-Empire attitude is apparent in his first despatch to *The Daily Telegraph*, which contained the following description of a seemingly-endless railway journey across India to the garrison town of Rawalpindi:

"At the station I was confronted by a fact which brings home with striking force the size of the Indian Empire. On asking the booking clerk - a sleek Babu - how far it was to Nowshera, he replied, with composure, that it was 2,027 miles. I rejoiced to think of the disgust with which a Little Englander would contemplate this fact. And then followed five weary days of train, the monotony of the journey only partially relieved by the changing scenes which the window presents.

Northwards, through the arid tracts that lie between Guntahal and Wadi Junction, through the green and fertile slopes of the Central Provinces, to more dry and unpropitious country at the foot of the great mountains, with the never-ceasing rattle of the railway irritating the nerves and its odious food cloying the palate, I am swiftly carried.

At Umballa a wing of the Dorsetshire Regiment is waiting, deterred from moving to Peshawar by several cholera cases; a few rest-camps near the line, a few officers hurrying to join their regiments, half-a-dozen nursing sisters travelling north on an errand of mercy, are the only signs so far of the war. But as Rawalpindi is neared the scene displays more significant features. Long trains of transport show the incessant passage of supplies to the front. One, in particular, of camels presents a striking picture. Six or seven of these animals are crowded into an open truck. Their knees are bound to prevent them moving on the journey, and their long necks, which rise in a cluster in the middle, have a strange and ridiculous aspect. Sometimes, I am told, curiosity, or ambition, or restlessness, or some other cause induces a camel to break his bonds and stand up, and as there are several tunnels in the line, the spectacle of a headless 'oont' is sometimes to be seen when the train arrives at Rawalpindi".

From Rawalpindi, the journey continued to Nowshera, where the Malakand field force had established its operational base. Here, Winston finally left the railway and set off by jolting 'tonga' passing, en route, a large field hospital filled with *"more than three hundred poor fellows in the different wards"* who had succumbed to fear, dysentery and bullets. The different stages of the journey were marked by rest camps at Mardom, Jelala and Dargai, while *"dead transport animals lay by the roadside, their throats hurriedly cut"*.

"After Dargai the Malakand Pass is reached, and henceforth the road winds upwards, until a two hours' climb brings the tonga to rest beneath the hill on which the fort stands. The ground is as broken and confused as can be imagined. On every side steep and often precipitous hills, covered with boulders and stunted trees, rise in confused irregularity. A hollow in the middle - the crater - is the camp of the West Kent Regiment. The slopes are dotted with white tents perched on platforms cut in the side of the hill. On one of these platforms my own is now pitched, and its situation commands a view of the ground on which, a month ago the fighting took place. In front is the signal station - a strong tower held by a picket - from which all day long the heliograph is flickering and blinking its messages to Nowshera, India, and on to the tape machines at the London clubs".

Winston's First Book

The losses on the North-West Frontier were heavy, and for this reason Winston found himself posted to the 31st Punjab Infantry, of whose language he knew only three words, and served with them for the rest of the campaign till his leave from the Hussars had long expired. When he returned to Bangalore, Winston began writing a full account of the expedition, the result being his first book - *The Story of The Malakand Field Force*, which was published in 1898 and became a remarkable success, earning him the equivalent of two years' pay.

This first book established Winston's reputation as an able and original young author, and won him a warm letter of appreciation from the Prince of Wales. On the other hand, it was not welcomed quite so warmly in military circles - the Army high command being understandably annoyed that a junior officer should have criticised, so freely and with such utter confidence, the blundering incompetence of many of his superiors.

Winston the Medal-Seeker

All his life Winston seemed to believe that military service, medals and 'good war service' were essential ingredients for political success. This may explain, to some extent, his apparent eagerness to see action in Cuba, the North-West Frontier and other conflict zones. In truth, he was quite shameless in his quest for medals, and in a letter written from Inayat Khan on 2nd October 1897 he asked his mother make a 'fuss', in order that 'they may give a special clasp for the Mahmund Valley':

"My dearest Mamma,
Since I last wrote to you we have had another severe action, Agrah 30th September - 1 was under fire for five hours - but did not get into the hottest corners. Our loss was 60 killed and wounded out of the poor 1,200 we can muster. Compare these figures with actions like Firket in Egypt which are cracked up as great battles and which are commemorated by clasps & medals, etc., etc. Here out of one brigade we have lost in a fortnight 245 killed and wounded and nearly 25 officers.

I hope you will talk about this to the Prince and others - as if any fuss is made, they may give a special clasp for Mamund Valley. This has been the hardest fighting on the frontier for forty years. I have been attached, as a matter of extreme urgency—to 31st Punjab Infantry. A change from British cavalry to Native Infantry! Still it means the medal and also that next time I go into action I shall command a hundred men - and possibly I may bring off some 'coup'. Besides I shall have some other motive for taking chances than merely love of adventure.

Today and yesterday I have fever. 103 degrees and an awful head - but I hope to be alright tomorrow. We expect another action on the 5th - Sir Bindon Blood is coming up himself and bringing two more batteries and two fresh Battalions. The danger and difficulty of attacking these active, fierce hill men is extreme. They can get up the hills twice as fast as we can - and shoot wonderfully well with Martini Henry Rifles. It is a war without quarter".

The Fall of Khartoum

While the Frontier rebellion in India was still petering out, Winston learned of an impending war in an entirely different part of the Empire. In the early 1880s a major uprising had broken out in the Sudan, then a virtual appendage of Egypt, which had come within the British sphere of influence. The uprising was led by Mohammed Ahmed of Dongola, a fanatical Islamic religious leader who called himself 'The Mahdi' – the twelfth Imam or Expected One, whom many Moslems believed would herald the end of the world. An Egyptian army commanded by General

Bugle & Sabre Special

William Hicks had been sent to attack the Mahdists (or Dervishes), in 1881, but his makeshift force had been utterly defeated by the insurgents at Kashgil.

Following the setback at Kashgil, Gladstone's Liberal government decided that all Anglo-Egyptian forces would be withdrawn from the Sudan, the officer selected to organise this delicate operation being General Charles Gordon (1833-85), a brave but unorthodox leader, who soon found himself cut-off and besieged in the Sudanese capital of Khartoum. The Gladstonian Liberals, who were totally indifferent to the British Empire, refused to send a relieving expedition until it was too late and, as a result, General Gordon and his Egyptian garrison were overrun and massacred by the Dervishes on 26th January 1885.

With Egypt itself now threatened, the government was obliged to send further military expeditions to the Sudan. On 30th December 1885, Major-General Frances Grendell attacked the Dervish positions at Ginness. The resulting Anglo-Egyptian victory being of interest, in that The battle of Ginniss was the last occasion on which members of the British army fought in red coats – The South Staffordshire Regiment, Gordon Highlanders and other units having been ordered to wear their red tunics 'to look more formidable to the Dervishes'.

Winston & The Battle of Omderman

Although the Mahdi died shortly after the fall of Khartoum, The Sudan became a focus for Islamic unrest, and with the slave trade flourishing in the African interior, Horatio Herbert Kitchener (1850-1916) was appointed 'Sirdar', or commander, of the Egyptian army. In the next few years he began elaborate preparations for a renewed campaign in the Sudan. Fully supported by Lord Salisbury's Conservative administration, a major expedition was sent into the Sudan, and on 1st September a cavalry patrol led by Winston Churchill – who had obtained a commission with the 21st Lancers – became the first men to see the enormous Dervish army, at least 50,000 strong, drawn up on the Plain of Omderman, near Khartoum. He described his experiences as follows:

"We distinguished many horsemen riding about the flanks and front of the great dark line which crowned the crest of the slope. A few of these rode forward carelessly towards the watching squadrons to look at them. They were not apparently acquainted with the long range of the Lee-Metford carbine. Several troops were dismounted, and at eight hundred yards fire was made on them. Two were shot and fell to the ground. Their companions, dismounting, examined them, picked up one, let the other lie, and resumed their ride without acknowledging the bullets by even an increase of pace.

While this little incident passed so did the time. It was now nearly eleven o'clock. Suddenly the whole black line, which seemed to be zareba, began to move. It was made of men not bushes. Behind it other immense masses and lines of men appeared over the crest, and while we watched, amazed by the wonder of the sight, the whole face of the slope became black with swarming savages. Four miles from end to end, and in five great divisions, this mighty army advanced, and swiftly. The whole side of the hill seemed to move. Between the masses horsemen galloped continually. Before them many patrols dotted the plain, above them waved hundreds of banners, and the sun, glinting on perhaps forty thousand hostile spear-points, spread a sparkling cloud. It was, perhaps, the impression of a lifetime, nor do I expect ever again to see such an awe-inspiring and formidable sight. We estimated their number at not less than forty thousand men, and it is now certain fifty thousand would have been nearer the truth.

The steady and continuous advance of the great army compelled us to mount our horses and trot off to some safer point of view, while our patrols and two detached troops, engaging the Dervish scouts, opened a dropping fusillade. I was sent back to describe the state of affairs to the Sirdar, but as he had already witnessed the spectacle from the top of the black hill - Heliograph Hill I shall call it in future - you are the first to receive my account.

From the summit the scene was extraordinary. The great army of Dervishes was dwarfed by the size of the landscape to mere dark smears and smudges on the brown sand of the plain. Looking east another army was now visible - the British and Egyptian army. All three divisions had crossed the Kerreri position and now stood drawn up in formation for attack in a crescent, with their backs to the Nile. The transport and the houses of the village filled the enclosed space. I looked from one array to the other. That of the enemy was without doubt denser and longer. Yet there seemed a superior strength in the solid battalions, whose lines were so straight that they might have been drawn with a ruler. Neither force could see the other, though but five miles divided them.

At a quarter to two the Dervish army halted. Their drill appeared excellent, and they all stopped as by a single command. The nearest troops to them were the 21st Lancers, who were about a mile and a half away. We watched them anxiously, for if they continued to advance the action would have been brought on at once. No sooner had they halted than their riflemen discharged their rifles in the air with a great roar - a barbaric feu-de-joie. Then they all lay down on the ground, and it became evident that the matter would not be settled till the morrow".

On the following day, 2nd September 1898, 20,000 British and Egyptian troops confronted the Dervishes, Kitchener's artillery being used to devastating effect as the closely-packed tribesmen advanced towards the disciplined ranks of the Anglo-Egyptian infantry. Captain E. A. Stanton of the Oxfordshire Light Infantry, who was present at this famous battle, having been 'loaned' to the Egyptian army, recalled that the Dervish front extended across the horizon for upwards of four or five miles, and looked, as it advanced, like a living wall.

"It was an inspiriting, as well as an awe-inspiring site, to see this mass of humanity moving forward to certain death. At 6.30

our first gun boomed out, firing on the enemy's right, which was now swarming over the rocky slopes of Jebel Surgham on our left. Soon the whole of our artillery, together with the guns of the gunboats on each flank, joined in. The execution was splendid, and was answered by two of the enemy's guns on our left, and by a general fusillade all along his front. Two shells burst in camp, but most of his fire was going high, though there were numerous casualties, more particularly among the British Brigades, who were receiving the first attack. The latter were now hard at work; well-directed volleys were being poured in; Maxims were raining sheets of lead; shrapnels were bursting in all directions, and whole lines of the enemy were being simply wiped away, while great gaps kept appearing in their close-serried ranks. Still on they came undismayed, advancing up to within 400 yards, beyond which all who attempted to advance were speedily shot down".

Meanwhile, on another part of the battlefield, Winston was also observing the steady advance of the vast Dervish army, their Emirs galloping about, while the black flag of the Khalifa floated high above their centre. As he watched the attack develop, the enemy right seemed to be moving directly towards him - a mass of 7,000 men in perfect array, displaying a *"great number of flags, perhaps five hundred, which looked at the distance white, though they were really covered with texts from the Koran"*. He thought that the Khalifa's army looked like a scene from the Bayeaux Tapestry:

"Yet another body of the enemy, who had been drawn up behind the 'white flagmen', was moving slowly towards the Nile, echeloned still further behind their right, and not far from the suburbs of Omdurman. These men had evidently been posted to prevent the Dervish army being cut off from the city, and it was these that the 21st Lancers charged and drove back about two hours later. My attention was distracted from their movements by the loud explosion of artillery. The Dervish centre had come into range, and the batteries opened on them. Above the heads of the moving masses shells began to burst, dotting the air with smoke balls and the ground with bodies. But they were nearly two miles away, and the distance rendered me unsympathetic.

I looked back to the 'white flagmen'. They were very nearly over the crest. In another minute they would become visible to the batteries. Did they realise what would come to meet them? They were in a dense mass scarcely two thousand yards from the 32nd Field Battery and the gunboats. The ranges were known. It was a matter of machinery. The more distant cannonade passed unnoticed as the mind concentrated on the impending horror. I could see it coming. It was a matter of seconds, and then swift destruction would rush on these brave men".

The first Dervish attack having been totally annihilated, Kitchener ordered the army to advance towards Omdurman, but it soon became clear that the Dervishes had not yet been defeated, and the Anglo-Egyptian force came under renewed attack. Thousands of tribesmen were again mowed down by sustained fire from those 'powerful weapons of civilisation – the shrapnel shell, the magazine rifle and the Maxim gun'. The one-sided contest was again witnessed at first hand by Captain Stanton, who recalled that 'The shooting of the guns and the Maxims was simply splendid. Shell after shell burst with the most wonderful precision right among the advancing hordes, making wide gaps, which were quickly filled from behind'.

At about 8.40 am, the 21st Lancers were ordered to advance towards the Dervish right, in order to cut off their retreat towards Omderman. As they rode towards a what appeared to be small group of enemy riflemen, it became apparent that there were in fact many more Dervishes in a hidden nullah or desert ravine. *"The riflemen were but a trifle compared to what lay behind. In a deep fold of the ground - completely concealed by its peculiar formation - a long, dense, white mass of men became visible".*

There were perhaps as many as 4,000 Dervishes in the ravine but, undeterred, the 400 Lancers proceeded to charge the enemy, and Winston thereby became a participant in the last classic cavalry charge in British military history:

"The Lancers acknowledged the unexpected sight only by an increase of pace. A desire to have the necessary momentum to drive through so solid a line animated each man. But the whole affair was a matter of seconds. At full gallop and in the closest order the squadron struck the Dervish mass. The riflemen, who fired bravely to the last, were brushed head over heel in the khor. And with them the Lancers jumped actually on to the spears of the enemy, whose heads were scarcely level with the horses' knees.

It is very rarely that stubborn and unshaken infantry meet equally stubborn and unshaken cavalry. Usually, either the infantry run away and are cut down in flight, or they keep their heads and destroy nearly all the horsemen by their musketry. In this case the two living walls crashed together with a mighty collision. The Dervishes stood their ground manfully. They tried to hamstring the horses. They fired their rifles, pressing the muzzles into the very bodies of their opponents. They cut bridle-reins and stirrup-leathers. They would not budge till they were knocked over. they stabbed and hacked with savage pertinacity. In fact, they tried every device of cool determined men practised in war and familiar in cavalry. Many horses pecked on landing and stumbled in the press, and the man that fell was pounced on by a dozen merciless foes. The regiment broke completely through the line everywhere, leaving sixty Dervishes dead and many wounded in their track. A hundred and fifty yards away they halted, rallied, and in less than five minutes were reformed and ready for a second charge".

Kitchener's army entered Omderman on 2nd September and formally occupied it on the following day. On 4th September they took possession of Khartoum and hoisted the Union flag over the city. Winston was shocked and saddened to see hundreds of wounded

Dervishes still lying on the sun-baked battlefield, no less than three days after the engagement, and he described how a fellow officer had offered water to some of the dying tribesmen:

"There may have been wounded Dervish among the heaps of slain. The atmosphere forbade approach. There certainly were many scattered about the plain. We approached these cautiously, and pistol in hand examined their condition. Lord Tullibardine had a large water-bottle. He dismounted and gave a few drops to each till all was exhausted. You must remember that this was three days after the fight, and that the sun had beaten down mercilessly all the time. Some of the wounded were very thirsty. It would have been a grateful sight to see a large bucket of clear, cool water placed before each shaking feverish figure. That, or a nameless man with a revolver and a big bag of cartridges, would have seemed merciful.

The scenes were pathetic. Where there was a shady bush four men had crawled to die. Someone had spread a rag on the thorns to increase the shade. Three of the unfortunate creatures had attained their object. The fourth survived. He was shot through both legs. The bullet - a Martini-Henry bullet - had lodged in the right knee-cap. The whole limb was stiffened. We gave him a drink. You would not think such joy could come from a small cup of water. Tullibardine examined his injury. Presently he pulled out his knife, and after much probing and cutting extracted the bullet - with the button-hook. I have seen, and shall see perhaps again, a man with a famous name worse employed".

The Start of the Boer War

When Winston went home to England at the end of the Omderman campaign he spent a few weeks in London before returning to India, where his regiment was attempting to win the All-India Cavalry Cup – a prestigious polo trophy. In the summer of 1899 he tried, unsuccessfully, to win his first political contest in the Oldham by-election. By that time, however, a further colonial war was brewing in southern Africa, and Winston was soon involved in this new conflict – which would win him further fame and fortune.

The origins of the Boer War were complex, but can be summarised as follows. Long-established Dutch settlements at the southern tip of Africa had been conquered by the British in 1806 and ceded to Britain under the provisions of the Treaty of Vienna in 1815. Unfortunately, the Dutch settlers, known as the 'Boers', disliked the British, and in the 1830s many of them 'trekked', or migrated northwards from Cape Colony into the veldt, where they founded new colonies on the Orange River and in Natal. The uneasy relationship between the British and Boer settlers in South Africa was upset by the discovery of gold in the Boer republic of the Transvaal in 1886, after which 'Uitlanders', or foreigners, many of them British, flocked into the goldfields and threatened the distinctive way of life of the Boer farmers. A period of rising tension culminated in the outbreak of war between Britain and the Boer republics on 12th October 1899.

The first phase of the conflict was marked by a series of Boer victories. Britain had very few regular troops in South Africa, and most of these became trapped in the besieged towns of Mafeking, Kimberley and Lady Smith. Following the arrival of British reinforcements at the end of October, General Sir Redvers Buller, the Commander-in-Chief, tried unsuccessfully to relieve Kimberley and Lady Smith. His efforts resulted in 'Black Week' between 10th and 15th December, when General Gatacre was defeated at Stormberg, Lord Methuen was defeated at Magersfontein and General Buller was repulsed at Colenso.

The Highest-Paid War Correspondent

Winston, who had by now decided to pursue a career in politics, resigned his commission in the summer of 1899. Thus, when the Boer War broke out in that same year, he was a civilian – although he was able to arrange a contract with *The Morning Post* which enabled him to enter the war zone as a war correspondent. His salary, of £250 per month, with all expenses paid, made him the highest-paid war correspondent in South Africa. A fellow-journalist, who sailed with Winston from Southampton to Cape Town aboard the *RMS Dunottar Castle*, described him as follows;

"He was slim, slightly reddish-haired, pale, lively, frequently plunging along the deck 'with neck out-thrust' as Browning fancied Napoleon ... when the prospects of a career like that of his father, Lord Randolph, excited him, then such a gleam shone from him that he was almost transfigured. I had not before encountered this sort of ambition, unabashed, frankly egotistical, communicating its excitement, and extorting sympathy".

The Armoured Train Incident

The *Dunottar Castle* docked at Cape Town on 31st October 1899, and Winston then made his way to Durban. There seemed, at first, to be few signs of war although, hoping to see the army in action, he obtained a lift on the Estcourt armoured train. Railways featured prominently in the Boer War. The army had, since the outbreak of hostilities, relied heavily on the South African railway system for the movement of troops and equipment – indeed, the Boers claimed that the British 'never leave the railway because they cannot march'. Railway bridges were frequently destroyed by the Boers and, in an attempt to prevent these troublesome raids, armoured patrol trains were brought into use.

The Estcourt train was formed of five vehicles, the leading vehicle being an ordinary goods wagon carrying an obsolete 9-pounder muzzle-loading gun manned by sailors from *HMS Tarter*, while the second vehicle was an armoured bogie wagon containing members of the Dublin Fusiliers. These two vehicles were marshalled in

A contingent of Royal Dublin Fusiliers climb aboard an armoured train during the Boer War. This photograph is said to have been taken at Estcourt on 15th November 1899.
Oxfordshire & Buckinghamshire Light Infantry Museum

A rare glimpse of the inside of an armoured bogie wagon during the Boer War.
Oxfordshire & Buckinghamshire Light Infantry Museum

A Maxim gun mounted on a land carriage during the Boer War. When he was under fire during the armoured train incident Winston clearly remembered 'the shell-firing Maxim ... and its little shells, discharged with a ugly thud, thud, thud', and exploding with 'startling bangs on all sides'.
Oxfordshire & Buckinghamshire Light Infantry Museum

front of the locomotive so that, on the outward journey from Estcourt, the gun wagon was at the very front of the ensemble. The three trailing vehicles comprised two more armoured bogie wagons manned by the Dublin Fusiliers and the Durham Light Infantry, together with a general purpose wagon carrying tools and track maintenance equipment.

On 15th November, the train, commanded by Captain Aylmer Haldane (1862-1950), set out on a reconnaissance mission in the direction of Colonso, but on arrival at Chieveley, some 16 miles from Estcourt, it was ordered to return to Frere, as parties of Boers could be seen on the horizon. Unfortunately, as the armoured train reversed hurriedly towards Frere, it ran into a large boulder which the Boers had placed across the track, three of the wagons being derailed. The maintenance wagon and one of the armoured wagons were thrown clear of the track, but the third wagon was slewed sideways and blocked the line.

The engine and two remaining wagons thereby became

An artist's impression of the armoured train ambush in which Winston was captured by the Boers. One of the bogie wagons is on its side, but the engine and tender remain on the rails. The Durham Light Infantry and the Royal Dublin Fusiliers are defending themselves against well-concealed Boer marksmen. *Oxfordshire & Buckinghamshire Light Infantry Museum*

trapped, but Winston, displaying an ice-cool nerve, organized a working party in an attempt to clear the debris from the line. Meanwhile, the Boers opened fire at 60 yards with rifles, three 15-pounder field guns, and a Maxim or 'pom-pom' gun. Winston and other members of the volunteer working party were fully exposed to the incessant enemy fire and, although unafraid, Winston clearly remembered *"the shell-firing Maxim .... and its little shells, discharged with a ugly thud, thud, thud"*, and exploding with *"startling bangs on all sides"*. Although the engine finally rammed the derailed wagon and escaped carrying a number of wounded men, Winston and most of those who had been aboard the train were captured by the Boers.

Winston Churchill VC?

It is perhaps ironic that Winston, who had shamelessly lobbied for medals on previous occasions when he had done little to earn them, was not awarded a medal for his unquestionable bravery during the armoured train incident. Many commentators suggested that he should have been recommended for a Victoria Cross, and the failure of the British authorities to offer him any form of decoration hints that Winston had already made many enemies in military circles. Leo Amery of *The Times*, J.B.Atkins of *The Manchester Guardian*, G.W.Steevens of *The Daily Mail* and Bennett Burleigh of *The Daily Telegraph* all agreed that Winston had acted with great gallantry, while on 17th November 1899 the following letter from Inspector Campbell of the Natal Government Railways to the General Manager of the Railway appeared in *The Natal Witness*:

"The railway men who accompanied the armoured train this morning ask me to convey to you their admiration of the coolness and pluck displayed by Mr Winston Churchill, the war correspondent who accompanied the train and to whose efforts, backed up by those of the driver, Wagner, is due the fact that the armoured train and tender were successfully brought out, after being hampered by the derailed trucks in front, and that it became possible to bring the wounded in here. The whole of our men are loud in their praises of Mr Churchill, who I regret to say, has been taken prisoner. I respectfully ask you to convey their admiration to a brave man".

Escape From the Boers

Having been captured by the Boers, Winston and the other captives were marched across the veldt to the States Model School at Pretoria, which had been hastily-adapted for use as a prison camp. Much to Winston's surprise, the Boers were polite, and not unfriendly, but he bitterly resented becoming a prisoner, and was determined to escape. Pro-Boer elements later alleged that Winston broke his parole, having given his word to his captors that if he was released he would not take up arms against them, but as no promise of release was ever made, this

Above: Winston (on the right) after capture by the Boers. As a civilian who had taken part in military operations, he could possibly have been shot, but the Boers decided to treat him as an ordinary prisoner-of-war.
Imperial War Museum

Right: A copy of the £25 'Dead or Alive' notice circulated by the Boers after Winston's escape. The translation reads:

£25.-.-
(Twenty-five Pounds stg)
<u>Reward</u> is offered by the Sub-Commission of the fifth division, on behalf of the Special Constable of the said division, to anyone who brings the escaped prisoner of war
     Churchill
dead or alive to this office
For the Sub-Comm of the fifth division
(Signed) Lodk de Haas,
Sec.

Oxfordshire Yeomanry Trust

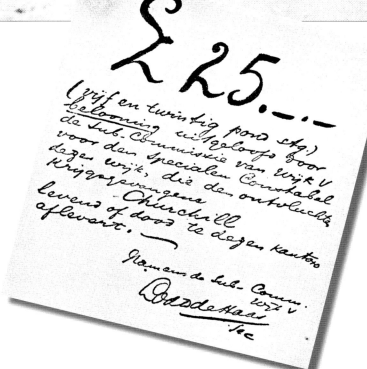

allegation would seem to be untrue.

Winston's dramatic escape from Pretoria was one of the most fantastic adventures in a life holding many thrilling experiences, although there was, perhaps, an element of truth in the suggestion that Winston, ever the opportunist, had persuaded Captain Haldane and Sergeant-Major Brockie to include him in their escape plan on the understanding that all three would leave together, and then climbed out of the enclosure on his own. After 'a series of adventures worthy of John Buchan's hero Richard Hannay', he eventually made his way to the safety of Lourenço-Marques in Portuguese East Africa by jumping aboard an eastbound freight train and hiding beneath sacks of potatoes and other merchandise until the train had safely crossed the border into neutral territory.

Winston's escape from the Boer prison camp delighted the public, who had become used to nothing but bad news from the war in South Africa. The story of the armoured train had already reached the press, and newspaper correspondents were full of praise for his gallant exploits. The wounded men who had escaped on the locomotive had already praised him generously, and news of Winston's triumphant return from the prison camp 'came like a ray of sunshine through the dense gloom of war reports' which would otherwise have been merely a succession of humiliating defeats. British residents at Lourenço-Marques formed an armed escort to take him down to the quayside from where he boarded a steamer for Durban, while on arrival at Durban – a loyalist stronghold - he was carried shoulder-high to the Town Hall, where the wildly cheering multitude insisted that he gave a speech.

The South African Light Horse

Winston, a national hero following his escape from the Boers, hurried back to the combat zone, where General Buller congratulated him and wanted to enrol him in the forces. However, as a result of the furore created by Winston's activities as an officer-correspondent during the Omderman campaign, serving officers in the British Army were forbidden to act as newspaper correspondents. As Winston refused to give up his lucrative contract with *The Morning Post*, it was decided that he would be given a commission in the South African Light Horse - an irregular unit distinguished by their plumed slouch hats, which had earned them the nick-name the 'Cockyoli Birds'. They were raised and commanded by Colonel Byng who, in later years, would be known as Lord Byng of Vimy – one of the most popular army commanders of World War I.

The Battle of Spion Kop

In January 1900, General Buller fought a disastrous and utterly futile battle at Spion Kop – the 'look-out hill' – in which over 2,000 British soldiers were left under murderous fire on an exposed hill-top position, while 10,000 of their comrades stood idly by. Winston, who was present during this infamous action and witnessed the senseless slaughter at first hand, left the following account of the most critical moments of the battle.

"Morning broke, and with it the attack. The enemy, realising the vital importance of the position, concentrated every man and every gun at his disposal for its recapture. A fierce and furious shell fire was opened forthwith on the summit, causing immediate and continual loss. General Woodgate was wounded, and the command devolved on a regimental officer who, at half-past six, applied for reinforcements in a letter which scarcely displayed that composure and determination necessary in such a bloody debate.

Sir Redvers Buller then took the extreme step of appointing major Thorneycroft - already only a local Lieutenant-Colonel - local brigadier-general commanding on the summit of Spion Kop. The Imperial Light Infantry, the Middlesex Regiment, and a little later the Somersets, from General Talbot Coke's brigade, were ordered to reinforce the defence, but General Coke was directed to remain below the summit of the hill, so that the fight might still be conducted by the brave men who were fighting.

The Boers followed, and accompanied their shells by a vigorous rifle attack on the hill, and about half-past eight the position became most critical. The troops were driven almost entirely off the main plateau and the Boers succeeded in re-occupying some of their trenches. A frightful disaster was narrowly averted. About twenty men in one of the captured trenches abandoned their resistance, threw up their hands and called out that they would surrender.

Colonel Thorneycroft, whose great stature made him everywhere conspicuous, and who was from dawn to dusk in the first firing line, rushed to the spot. The Boers advancing to take the prisoners – as at Nicholson Nek – were scarcely thirty yards away. Thorneycroft shouted to the Boer leader: 'You may go to hell. I command on this hill and allow no surrender. Go on with your firing'. Which latter they did with terrible effect, killing many. The survivors, with the rest of the firing line, fled two hundred yards, were rallied by their indomitable commander and, being reinforced by two brave companies of the Middlesex Regiment, charged back, recovering all lost ground, and the position was maintained until nightfall.

No words in these days of extravagant expression can do justice to the glorious endurance which the English regiments – for they were all English - displayed throughout the long dragging hours of shell fire. Between three and four o'clock the shells were falling on the hill from both sides, as I counted, at the rate of seven a minute, and the strange discharge of the Maxim shell guns – the 'pom-poms' as these terrible engines are called for want of a correct name – lacerated the hillsides with dotted chains of smoke and dust. A thick and continual stream of wounded flowed rearwards. A village of ambulance wagons grew up at the foot of the mountain. The dead and injured, smashed and broken by the shells, littered the summit till it was a bloody, reeking shambles".

Captain Cecil Boyle, wearing the full dress uniform of the Queens Own Oxfordshire Hussars. Captain Boyle was killed in action during the Boer War on 5th April 1900.
Oxfordshire Yeomanry Trust OXYT981

Winston at Ladysmith

On 10th January Lord Roberts had arrived in Cape Town to take over from the ineffective Buller as Commander-in-Chief, his Chief of Staff being the very capable Lord Kitchener of Khartoum. The results of this change of leadership were dramatic – Kimberley was relieved on 15th February, while General Pietrus Cronje's besieging forces soon found themselves trapped on the wrong side of the Modder River gorge at Paardeberg. The Boers took up defensive positions along the north bank. Attempts to dislodge them were repulsed with heavy losses, but British reinforcements were now appearing in large numbers, and having surrounded the Boers, Lord Roberts was able to shell them into submission – an unconditional surrender being agreed on 27th February 1900.

General Cronje's defeat disheartened the Boers, and they withdrew from Ladysmith, enabling Buller to enter the town on 28th February without opposition. Meanwhile, Kitchener had taken energetic steps to increase the mobility of his forces, an efficient system of wagon transport being organised to reduce dependence on the railways, while mounted infantry and Yeomanry units were employed to good effect in the vast open spaces of the veldt. On 13th March, Lord Roberts was able to occupy Bloemfontein, the capital of the Orange Free State, while on 28th May the British annexed the Orange Free State, re-naming it 'The Orange River Colony'. In that same month Lord Roberts occupied Johannesburg, while Pretoria was captured on 5th June. On 1st September Britain annexed the Boer republic of the Transvaal.

Winston managed to see action in various places during the next few months as he followed the British forces in their pursuit of the Boers. When the army reached Ladysmith he entered the beleaguered town with the first relief column on the evening of 28th February 1900. With him he brought a box of food which had been sent to him by his friend Miss Pamela Plowden, who had asked him to give it to her brother-in-law, Major Edgar Lafone. Unfortunately Major Lafone was not well enough to appreciate these delicacies and Winston had to report that he was *"impelled to eat them himself"*.

That night, he dined with the Sir George White, the defender of Ladysmith, while next to him sat Sir Ian Hamilton and next but one General Hunter. Conscious that he was taking part in a historic event, Winston commented, *"Never before have I sat in such brave company, nor stood so close to a great event"*. Following the relief of Ladysmith Winston obtained permission to join Lord Roberts as he advanced towards Johannesburg and Pretoria.

Winston The Peace-maker

Although, by 1900, the Boers had clearly been defeated in open battle and their republics annexed, the guerrilla war dragged on into 1902. Both sides were tired of a war that was expensive and humiliating for the British and disastrous for the Boers but, unfortunately, the Boers were deeply divided, insofar as the Free Staters refused to accept any peace settlement that did not guarantee their total independence, while the Boers of the Transvaal were prepared to compromise. Thus, when the British government sent a new offer to the Boers it appeared that the Transvaal was willing to talk, whereas the Free State insisted upon a fight to 'the bitter end'. In the event, after long drawn-out peace negotiations had run their tortuous course, both sides signed the Treaty of Vereeniging, which ended the war on 31st May 1902.

Winston had, at the start of the conflict in South Africa, disliked the Boers with a particular intensity, in part because he had heard stories of the 'horrible barbarities' that had been inflicted on native African refugees, who had been robbed, beaten and insulted by their European persecutors: *"One woman … had been flogged across the breasts, and was much lacerated. Such is the Boer – gross, fierce and horrid – doing the deeds of the devil with the name of the Lord on his lips. It is quite true that he is brave, but so are many savage tribes"*. At length, however, Winston made friends with individual Boer leaders such as Jan

Smuts and Louis Botha, and by the end of the war his attitude had become much more sympathetic. In his speeches and articles he urged that, as soon as victory was assured, a policy of generosity should dictate the terms of a peace settlement.

He argued that the British and Boers would have to live together when the fighting was over, and any display of vindictiveness in the hour of triumph would leave wounds in South Africa that might never heal. Sadly, Winston's wise and far-sighted vision was not shared by the British public, though in the next few years Winston was able to press for the granting of self-government for the Transvaal and Orange Free State, and these measures were successfully carried out in December 1906 and June 1907 respectively. In 1909 these two Boer colonies, together with Cape Colony and the largely-British colony of Natal, agreed to form The Union of South Africa as a self-governing Dominion within the British Empire.

Winston & Louis Botha

After Winston had helped to free the trapped locomotive during the armoured train incident, it was decided that the engine would return to Estcourt carrying the wounded, while the able-bodied would attempt to keep pace by running alongside. Inevitably, Winston was soon left behind, with the result that he was confronted, in a lonely railway cutting, by 'a tall, dark figure' on horseback, holding a rifle in his right hand. As he later recalled:

"I put my hand to my belt, the pistol was not there. When engaged in clearing the line, getting in and out of the engine, etc, I had taken it off: It came safely home on the engine I have it now! But at this moment I was quite unarmed. Meanwhile, I suppose in about the time this takes to tell, the Boer horseman, still seated on his horse, had covered me with his rifle. The animal stood stock still, so did he, and so did I. I looked towards the river, I looked towards the platelayers' hut. The Boer continued to look along his sights. I thought there was absolutely no chance of escape, if he fired he would surely hit me, so I held up my hands and surrendered myself a prisoner of war".

Winston thought no more about the tall dark Boer, but about three years later, when the Boer generals were visiting England to ask for financial assistance on behalf of their devastated country, he was introduced at a private luncheon to their leader, General Louis Botha:

"We talked of the war and I briefly told the story of my capture. Botha listened in silence; then he said, don't you recognise me? I was that man. It was I who took you prisoner. I, myself, and his bright eyes twinkled with pleasure. Botha in white shirt and frock coat looked very different in all save size and darkness of complexion from the wild war-time figure I had seen that rough day in Natal. But about the extraordinary fact there can be no doubt. He had entered upon the invasion of Natal as a burgher; his own disapproval of the war had excluded him from any high command at its outset. This was his first action. But as a simple private burgher serving in the ranks he had galloped ahead and in front of the whole Boer forces in the ardour of pursuit. Thus we met".

Further Books

Winston lost no time in turning his letters and despatches into further books, *The River War*, dealing with his experiences in the Omderman campaign, being published in 1899, while *London to Ladysmith via Pretoria*, which included the story of his escape from the Boers, and *Ian Hamilton's March* were both published in 1900. Other books published in the next few years included *Savrola* (1900), *Lord Randolph Churchill* (1906), *My African Journey* (1908) and *Liberalism & the Social Problem* (1910).

Origins of The Queens Own Oxfordshire Hussars

The Oxfordshire Yeomanry can be traced back to the 1790s, when fear of internal revolution coupled with fear of a French attack on Britain was so great that additional forces were raised for home defence purposes, Oxfordshire's main contribution being in the form of volunteer Yeoman cavalry units. In 1794 a meeting of 'Nobility, Gentry, Freeholders and Yeoman of the County' was held at the Star Inn in Oxford to discuss the raising of a troop of cavalry and, as a result, a regiment of cavalry was raised under the command of Colonel the Hon Thomas Parker.

By 1798, Oxfordshire could boast four troops of Yeoman cavalry, these units being known as The Watlington Troop, The Wootton Troop, The Bloxham & Banbury Troop and the Bullingdon, Dorchester & Thame Troop. Three more troops were subsequently formed, including a Woodstock Troop, which was intimately connected with Blenheim and successive Dukes of Marlborough.

The British armed forces were reduced in size after the final defeat of Napoleon in 1815 but, like other Yeomanry units, The Oxfordshire Yeomanry remained in being as a part-time, volunteer cavalry unit. In 1835 the Woodstock Troop of the Oxfordshire Yeomanry was re-titled 'The Queen's Own Royal Oxfordshire Yeomanry Cavalry' after they had escorted Queen Adelaide, the wife of William IV, during a visit to Oxford. At that time, the Yeomanry was regarded as a politically-reliable force of predominantly-Tory farmers which could be used to maintain public order in the absence of a police force. Mocking critics sometimes called them 'The Agricultural Cavalry'!

A Most Distinctive Uniform

As fears of social upheaval subsided during the long summer of Victorian prosperity, the Queens Own Oxfordshire Hussars came into their own as a largely-ceremonial organisation that reflected the social aspirations of great landed magnates such as the Churchills. The word 'Royal' had been quietly dropped by 1855, but in 1881 the regiment was re-titled 'The Queens Own

Oxfordshire Hussars'. As a corollary of this change of title the regiment had, between 1856 and 1863, adopted Hussar-style braided tunics and plumed busbies.

At the end of the Victorian period, the full-dress uniform of the Queens Own Oxfordshire Hussars included a black tunic with elaborate silver braiding on the chest, collar and sleeves and mantua purple facings – mantua purple, the Churchill family colour, having been a particular favourite of Queen Adelaide. The trousers were also mantua purple, with a silver stripe on each leg and additional silver braid on the front above each knee. The black fur busby was adorned with a purple busby bag, a tall plume of vulture ostrich feathers and a silver chinstrap. The highly polished Hessian boots had silver edging on the top with a purple boss and pink heels, while the sabretache, or dispatch case, was edged with silver lace and red piping – this most distinctive uniform being ideal for use at levees, balls and parades.

The Queens Own Oxfordshire Hussars service dress uniform was of dark blue serge with cavalry shoulder chains in place of epaulettes, the officers peaked service caps being mantua purple cloth with a black leather brim, silver buttons and the regimental insignia in white metal on the front. The regimental badge was made of white metal, brass or bronze and featured the 'AR' cypher of Queen Adelaide below an 'Adelaide' crown. Contemporary photographs often show Winston or other QOOH officers wearing white corduroy dust covers over their hats in order to keep them clean when outdoors.

Winston Joins the Oxfordshire Yeomanry

By the final decades of the Victorian period, the Queens Own Oxfordshire Hussars had become an integral part of the social scene at Blenheim and other great houses within the county – the extravagant Hussar uniforms, with their black tunics and purple-red trousers, being proudly worn at balls, soirées and other formal occasions. By this time, a number of ex-regular officers, such as Lord Valentia, had joined the QOOH and they were determined to give the regiment a more professional polish. This was achieved by the introduction, as instructors, of numbers of experienced NCOs and Warrant Officers on their retirement from the regular cavalry. Their efforts were undoubtedly successful, and young Winston would clearly have seen and admired the Oxfordshire Yeomanry during his innumerable visits to Blenheim. It is easy to understand the appeal of such a colourful force to an impressionable child with a love of military history.

As a young man, Winston had never thought of joining the Queens Own Oxfordshire Hussars – he was, in any case, a member of the Harrow Volunteer Rifle Corps, and although this would not have debarred him form accepting a commission in the Oxfordshire Yeomanry, he may have considered that this course of action would have been inappropriate.

In 1899, he tried to obtain a commission in the Royal Bucks Yeomanry before sailing to South Africa, his formal application being sent with a personal appeal to the Honorary Colonel – Lord Chesham. The application was never forwarded, for when he got on board ship he discovered that it would be easier to obtain a Yeomanry commission from the Adjutant of the 9th Yeomanry Brigade which was under the command of his father's old friend Lord Gerard of the Lancashire Hussars.

In 1901, the presence in the Regiment of many members fresh from service in the Boer War must have given a 'professional' tone to the Queens Own Oxfordshire Hussars, which may have engendered a renewed interest in Winston's mind. While this would also have applied to many other Yeomanry Regiments, it is clear from regimental records that Winston played a very significant part in increasing the professionalism of the QOOH before 1914 up to a point where it was at its very peak immediately before the outbreak of the Great War.

Service with the Woodstock Squadron

Documents in the Oxfordshire Yeomanry Collection reveal that Winston's association with the Queens Own Oxfordshire Hussars lasted for a much longer period than had hitherto been assumed, while he was also far more active and deeply involved than had been supposed. He first appeared with the rank of captain as second-in-command of the Woodstock Squadron on 19th November 1901 – his rank and appointment reflecting past service with the regular Cavalry. A photograph taken at that time shows him wearing a distinctly un-regimental uniform, comprising a khaki service jacket, a broad-brimmed bush hat with upturned side and a civilian-style bow tie. Winston was, at this time, not long back from his journalistic and semi-military exploits in South Africa, and he apparently wanted to emphasise this fact by wearing the distinctive uniform of the South African Light Horse.

Winston & The Henley Squadron

The Woodstock Squadron was at that time commanded by Winston's cousin Charles, but despite (or perhaps because of!) the dominant family interest in the Woodstock Squadron, Winston's name appeared on the strength of the Henley Squadron as soon as 4th January 1902 - his address in the Henley drill-record being given as 105, Mount Street London W1.

This London address hints at another reason for the transfer from Woodstock to Henley. On 1st May 1900 the Great Western Railway had introduced a much-improved train service on the Henley-on-Thames branch line and, as a result, the prosperous, riverside town of Henley was brought within one hour's travelling time of Paddington. Two trains, the 9.15 pm up service from Henley and the 10.00 am down from Paddington accomplished their journey in just 50 minutes. Travel from Mayfair to Henley for a day or evening drill session would thus have been entirely practicable, whereas similar journeys to and

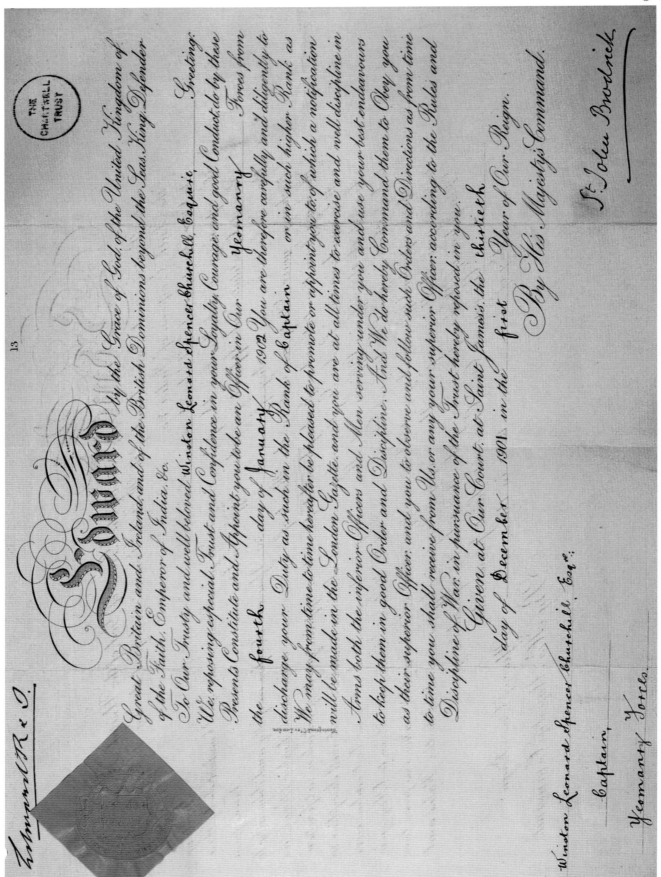

Winston's commission as a captain in the Queens Own Oxfordshire Hussars, dated 30th December 1901, and effective from 4th January 1902. Oxfordshire Yeomanry Trust

A group photograph showing officers from the QOOH and other regiments, probably at Blenheim circa 1901. Winston Churchill is featured wearing a slouch hat and bow tie – his Boer War uniform as a member of the South African Light Horse. Others present include Sir Robert Herman-Hodge (with large moustache) and the Duke of Marlborough.

Oxfordshire Yeomanry Trust OXYT654

from Blenheim & Woodstock station, with its infrequent branch line train service, would have taken somewhat longer.

Winston's service with the Henley Squadron, which extended from January 1902 until at least 1913, was his principal 'active' contribution to the Regiment. We do not, unfortunately, have an exact date for the end of his active participation, but we do know that he was still with the Squadron after he became First Lord of the Admiralty in October 1911 – indeed, on one occasion he took the entire Squadron to see the fleet at Portsmouth! Twelve years of active involvement is a long time for any Territorial to serve, and to be in command of a particular Squadron for eight years must be regarded as very unusual.

Absence from Annual Camp

Generally speaking, Winston was a highly-conscientious officer, though on 8th May 1904 he wrote to Regimental Headquarters requesting to be excused from attending the annual Yeomanry camp, citing 'grounds of political business and state affairs'. The camp was, in that year, held at South Park, Oxford, which was part of the Headington Hill estate and the home of the famous Oxford brewing family.

It is not entirely clear why he should have missed the annual camp in that particular year. It is possible that Winston's enthusiasm for the Queens Own Oxfordshire Hussars was not yet fully developed. Alternatively, the explanation could be simply that Winston, who had recently joined the Liberals, may have been reluctant to ask for leave from his 'day job' at a time when he was not yet fully established as a member of the Liberal Party. (Important as his political duties undoubtedly were 1904, they were no less demanding than in previous and subsequent years).

After 1904, however, notwithstanding his tenure in the Government of a number of great Offices of State, Winston's commitment to the Regiment and to the Henley Squadron appeared to grow. On 28th April 1905 he assumed command of the Squadron with the rank of Captain, while promotion to Major followed just one

Members of the Queens Own Oxfordshire Hussars let their horses drink from the Great Lake at Blenheim during a summer Yeomanry camp during the early 1900s. Summer training camps were held at Blenheim in 1901, 1903, 1905, 1906, 1911 and 1912.
Oxfordshire Yeomanry Trust OXYT650

Officers of the Queens Own Oxfordshire Hussars during their annual camp at Blenheim in 1901. Although Blenheim was the usual venue for Yeomanry training camps during the period 1900-1914, other venues included Fawley Park near Henley, Headington Hill, Wytham Park and Barley Hill Park near Thame.
Oxfordshire Yeomanry Trust OXYT580

A selection of menus, invitations and other ephemera reflecting the very full social life of the Henley Squadron during the Edwardian period. *Oxfordshire Yeomanry Trust*

Q.O.O. HUSSARS,

(Imperial Yeomanry).

HENLEY SQUADRON.

The Squadron will parade in Drill Order for Mounted Squadron Drills as follows:—

(1.) May 3rd.
" 10th.
" 24th. } On Bix Common, at 4.30 p.m. each day, the party from Henley will parade near the Drill Hall at 4 p.m.

" 8th.
" 20th. } At Thame, near the Town Hall, at 4 p.m. each day.

" 8th.
" 22nd. } At Coombe Park, at 4 p.m. each day.

I hope every member of the Squadron will do his utmost to attend these Mounted Parades.

(2.) Musketry Target Practice for all Members who did not attend the Shooting in August, 1904; also for all members who have joined since that date, will take place as follows:

May 17th.
" 18th. } On the Fair Mile Range, Henley, shooting to commence at 2 p.m each day.

(3.) A Shooting Competition will be held on 31st May, on the Fair Mile Range, commencing at 2 p.m.; 7 shots each at 200 and 400 yards. First prize, £2; Second prize, £1; Third prize, 15s.; Fourth prize, 10s. Marksmen will be handicapped 4 points, first-class shots 2 points.

All Members are invited to attend the Range on the 17th and 18th May, for Practice.

ALWYN FOSTER,
Captain,
Commanding Henley Squadron, Q.O.O.H.

Squadron Orders 'inviting' members of the Henley Squadron to attend mounted drills on Bix Common, Henley, at Thames and at Coombe Park, and musketry target practice on the Fair Mile Range at Henley. There was also to be a shooting competition on the Fair Mile Range. *Oxfordshire Yeomanry Trust*

month later, the entry in *The London Gazette* being as follows:

War Office
30th May 1905.

IMPERIAL YEOMANRY
Oxfordshire (Queens Own Oxfordshire Hussars)
The undermentioned officers to be Majors:
Captain W.L.S.Churchill. Dated 25th May 1905

From November 1905 until November 1909 the orders issued to the Henley Squadron were all headed 'By Major W. L. Spencer Churchill MP', although they were signed by Captain Alwyn Foster. It seems likely that Captain Foster was acting in the role of what would today be known as a Permanent Staff Administrative Officer (PSAO). He appears in some of the Regimental photographs, and was probably either a retired or seconded regular cavalry officer who had been tasked to ensure the smooth running of the Squadron and supervise training to professional standards. It is not clear whether all of the QOOH squadrons had the benefit of such expert help, but he clearly assumed much of the burden of running the unit.

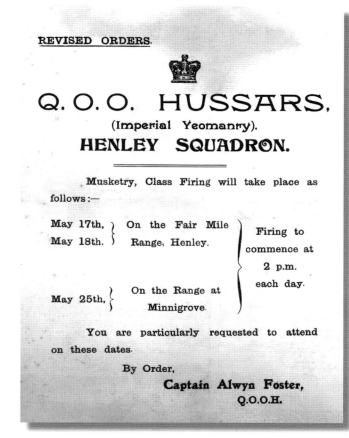

Squadron Orders for the Henley Squadron, again to attend musketry class firing on the ranges at Henley and Minnigrove. *Oxfordshire Yeomanry Trust*

The Top Squadron

From 4th April 1910 Captain Foster no longer signed the orders, which were sent out with the legend 'by order W. L. Spencer Churchill, Major' as well as being headed to the same effect. This seems to imply a deeper commitment by Winston, though it is unclear if Captain Foster had been replaced as PSAO, or if the squadron commander was responding to a regimental edict. In any event, from now on the intensity of the training can be seen from the orders issued to be relentlessly increasing. Not only were there additional pre-camp mounted drills – there was also extra musketry practice, sometimes up to twice a week from 2.00 pm until 5.00 pm from June to August.

This must have been a substantial imposition on volunteer Yeomen soldiers with civilian 'day jobs', but the extra training brought evident results, and in 1910 and again in 1911 the Henley Squadron swept the board at the Annual Regimental Musketry Meetings. As the culmination of all this effort, the Henley Squadron, under Winston, was selected from the whole of the British Yeomanry to manoeuvre with the Regular Cavalry, including the Household Brigade, on Salisbury Plain from 14th to 24th September 1911. This additional and hard-won commitment must have been regarded as a great accolade, and the records imply that Winston recognised the possibility and had worked his Squadron up in order to achieve it. It is, of course, conceivable that the idea of the manoeuvres with the regulars was Winston's in the first place, which makes the occurrence no less interesting.

Winston also played a full part in the intense social life of the Squadron during his tour in command. There were, for instance, Balls and Dinners in great country houses, sometimes two a year – these prestigious events being well recorded in the local press as high-points in the social calendar.

The 1908 Haldane Army Reforms

British reverses at the start of the Boer War had underlined the need for reform of the nation's armed forces, and in this context the changes initiated by Richard Haldane, the Minister of State for War in Herbert Asquith's Liberal government, were designed to save money and increase efficiency by creating a small, but effective regular army that could be quickly reinforced. To this end, he reduced size of the regular army by 16,600 men, while providing for an expeditionary force of 100,000 men that could be rushed to the Continent to face an enemy which was assumed to be Germany.

To facilitate this new plan, the militia regiments were formed into the 'Special Reserve', while the Volunteers and Yeomanry became the 'Territorial Force'. These changes were seen as an alternative to conscription – a measure that would have been anathema to the radicals and vociferous 'Little Englander' elements within Haldane's own party. Implicit in this new scheme was the idea that the newly-created 'Territorials' would be expected to serve overseas – albeit on a voluntary basis.

Q.O.O. HUSSARS,
HENLEY SQUADRON.

Orders by Major W. L. Spencer Churchill, M.P.

Annual Training. 1.—The Regiment will assemble for Annual Training at Blenheim Park. Woodstock, on 26th May to 9th June, 1911.

Pay. 2.—The issue of Pay and allowances during Annual Training will depend upon fulfilment of the conditions laying down the number of Recruit and Squadron Drills to be performed before attending the Annual Training.

Horses. 3.—On arrival in Camp, all horses will be inspected by a Board of Officers as to their soundness and fitness for Military Duty. No allowance will be paid for a horse that has not passed. Officers and men who bring their own horses to Training will be allowed compensation for the loss through death, destruction, or fatal injury on the same conditions as formerly. No compensation will be allowed for the temporary loss of an animal's services or for deterioration in its value.
No claim will be entertained for the repayment of Veterinary expenses necessary after the termination of the Training. On no account will horses under four years of age be passed as fit for Training. Each man will be held responsible that his horse is properly shod on arrival at Camp.

Dress. 4.—N.C.O's and men must not appear at any time during Training in Plain Clothes, or in any uniform, or appointments that are not strictly in accordance with the Regulations.
All blue clothing must be taken to Camp, and each man must be in possession of Dress Boots and one pair of White Kid Gloves.

Blankets. 5.—Blankets at the rate of two for each man and one for each horse will be provided. N.C.O's and men are recommended to bring an extra blanket for themselves.

Losses. 6.—The attention of all ranks is called to the excessive number of losses in the Camp Equipment during last Training.

Dogs. 7.—Dogs are not to be taken to or kept in Camp.

Postal Arrangements. 8.—Letters should be addressed—
Q.O.O. HUSSARS, Blenheim Park, Woodstock.

March Route. 9.—The Squadron will parade in marching order on the 26th May, and proceed by march route to Woodstock as follows:—
The Henley Troop, under Capt. C. R. I. Nicholl, will parade in the Market Place, at 7.45 a.m., moving off at 8 a.m., and will march via Benson, Dorchester and Littlemore, arriving there at noon. A halt will be made at Littlemore for watering and feeding.
The Goring Troop, under Lieut. V. Fleming, M.P., will assemble at Braziers Park, at 8.45 a.m, they will march via Mongewell, Wallingford to Shillingford, joining the Head-quarters there about 10 15 a.m
The Watlington Troop (except the Chinnor detachment), under Sergt. R. W. Buswell, will join the Head-quarters at Dorchester about 10.30 a m.
The Thame Troop (with the Chinnor detachment), under Capt. Lord Camoys, will parade in the Market Place, at 9 a m., and will march via Wheatley, Stanton, St. John and Islip.
Men travelling by rail will make their own arrangements for conveyances. Cattle truck rate only is allowed. Men using horse boxes must pay the difference of fare at the time of booking. N.C.O's and men intending to travel by rail must notify S.S.M. Collier not later than the 19th May.

WINSTON L. SPENCER CHURCHILL, Major,
Commanding Henley Company.

Detailed Squadron Orders issued by Major Winston L. Spencer Churchill in connection with the annual training camp which was held at Blenheim between 26th May and 9th June 1911. It will be noted that men were allowed to travel by rail at 'cattle truck rate' – those opting to travel by horse box being asked to pay the difference in fare at the time of booking. Blenheim & Woodstock station, which was sited in convenient proximity to Blenheim Park, was equipped with loading docks and horse landings to facilitate the transport of horses and carriages.
Oxfordshire Yeomanry Trust

An Oxfordshire Yeomanry church parade held at Blenheim Palace in company with the Royal Bucks Hussars and the Berkshire Yeomanry in 1911.
Oxfordshire Yeomanry Trust OXYT908

The Oxfordshire Yeomanry encamped at Blenheim, with the Column of Victory in the background.
Oxfordshire Yeomanry Trust OXFYT1071

A group photograph showing Winston Churchill and other members of the Henley Squadron in 1911. *Oxfordshire Yeomanry Trust OXYT279*

Oxfordshire Yeoman at their camp in Blenheim Park in 1912. *Oxfordshire Yeomanry Trust OXFYT976*

A group of Oxfordshire Yeomen with an 'F. W. Hedderly' wagon and civilian driver at Blenheim during the annual camp in 1912. Hedderly was Frederick William Hedderly, a job master and owner of a shoeing forge in Oxford.
Oxfordshire Yeomanry Trust OXYT979

Oxfordshire Yeoman Sam Joslin List on horseback while attending an annual Yeomanry training camp.
Oxfordshire Yeomanry Trust OXYT1053

A mass 'charge' of the Yeomanry during an annual summer camp. At the 1911 camp, the QOOH were brigaded with the Buckinghamshire Yeomanry, and Winston persuaded the commanding general to order the entire brigade, some 1,200 strong, to gallop the entire length of the park – a memorable sight for members of the public watching the event!
Oxfordshire Yeomanry Trust OXYT1097

Q.O.O. HUSSARS.

HENLEY SQUADRON.

The Annual Course of Musketry will be carried out as follows:—

INSTRUCTIONAL PRACTICES

At Maidens Grove, Bix Bottom, near Nettlebed,

June 21st, 28th, 29th; July 12th, 13th, 20th, 26th; August 2nd, 3rd, 17th.

Firing will commence at 2 p.m. each day.

"Standard Tests" will take place 19th and 27th July, commencing at 10.30 a.m. The dates for the other Standard Tests will be notified later.

All Rifles, complete with pull-throughs, oil bottles and slings, to be returned to Stores on conclusion of the course of Musketry.

It is notified for information that the Regimental Rifle Meeting will be held during the last week in July at Bicester.

All ranks are invited to attend the Range for practice any day that firing is taking place.

All Saddles, thoroughly clean and complete, to be returned to Stores without delay.

W. L. SPENCER CHURCHILL, M.P.,
Commanding Henley Squadron.

June, 1911.

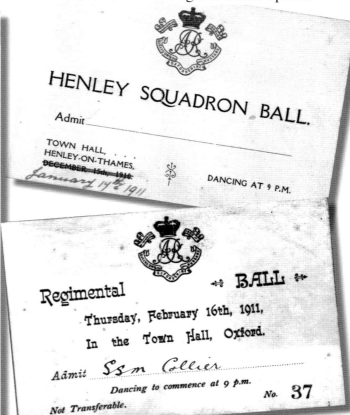

HENLEY SQUADRON BALL.

Admit _____

TOWN HALL,
HENLEY-ON-THAMES,
~~December 15th, 1910.~~
January 19th 1911

DANCING AT 9 P.M.

Regimental BALL

Thursday, February 16th, 1911,

In the Town Hall, Oxford.

Admit *SSM Collier*

Dancing to commence at 9 p.m.

Not Transferable.   No. 37

By permission of Lt.-Col. The Duke of Marlborough, K.G., Commanding Q.O.O.H.

The Annual Ball

OF THE

HENLEY SQUADRON,

Queen's Own Oxfordshire Hussars

will be held in the

TOWN HALL, HENLEY-ON-THAMES,

On Wednesday, December 11th, 1912.

HENLEY SQUADRON
QUEEN'S OWN OXFORDSHIRE HUSSARS.

ANNUAL BALL,

under the distinguished Patronage of Col. His Grace the DUKE OF MARLBOROUGH, K.G., and the Officers of the Regiment, will be held in the

TOWN HALL, HENLEY-ON-THAMES,

ON WEDNESDAY, JANUARY 31st, 1912.

Dancing to Commence at 9 p.m.

COMMITTEE:

Major the Right Hon. Winston L. Spencer Churchill, M.P.

Capt. C. R. I. Nicholl.
Lieut. Val. Fleming, M.P.
Sergt. R. W. Buswell (Warborough).
 "   C. J. Buswell (Stadhampton).
 "   S. A. Wright (Nettlebed).
 "   E. M. Potter (Thame).
Corpl. B. J. Smither (Woodcote).
Trooper J. Kibler (Henley-on-Thames).
 "   J. R. Ashford (Henley-on-Thames).

Capt. The Lord Camoys.
Lieut. P. Fleming.
Sergt. H. J. Saunders (Henley-on-Thames).
 "   W. G. Weyman (Henley-on-Thames).
 "   A. E. Batty (Henley-on-Thames).
Corpl. R. L. Wright (Henley-on-Thames).
 "   W. E. Roberts (Thame).
Trooper L. F. Gale (Wallingford).
 "   P. W. Hicks (Watlington).
Sergt.-Major A. Collier (Henley-on-Thames), Sec. and Treas.

Tickets may be obtained through any member of the Committee. An early application is requested.

TICKETS 7/6 EACH.

A further selection of ephemera relating to the activities of the Henley Squadron in the years before World War I.
Oxfordshire Yeomanry Trust

The programme for the Henley Squadron Annual Ball, which took place on 21st January 1914. *Oxfordshire Yeomanry Trust*

Winston & the QOOH in World War I

By August 1914 Winston had given up the command of the Henley Squadron. War in Europe was imminent following the assassination of the Austrian Arch-Duke Franz Ferdinand at Sarajevo and the Austrian ultimatum to Serbia on 24th July. As First Lord of the Admiralty, Winston's primary duties were clearly elsewhere, but his close interest in the Queens Own Oxfordshire Hussars nevertheless continued unabated. On 13th August, for example, Winston brought his friend General Sir Ian Hamilton, who was then Commander-in-Chief Land Forces UK, to dine with the officers of two Oxfordshire Hussar Squadrons at the Caversham Bridge Hotel, Reading.

A visit by a full General at the start of a major war can hardly have been merely a social occasion, and it is conceivable that Winston was hoping to persuade the General to take the Regiment with the British Expeditionary Force to France in their cavalry role. If so, that particular ploy did not succeed although, just one month later, Winston was asked in his capacity as First Lord of the Admiralty to send a detachment of Royal Marines to assist the French forces in the area around Dunkirk. Winston agreed to this request, but only on condition that the Marines were accompanied by a Yeomanry Regiment to act as their 'supporting cavalry'. Thus, on 20th September 1914, despite an initial lack of training and shortages of equipment, the Queens Own Oxfordshire Hussars found themselves on their way to France aboard the *SS Bellerophon* as part of the Royal Naval Division.

The Queens Own Oxfordshire Hussars were subsequently incorporated into the regular cavalry order of battle - one of few Yeomanry regiments to be so treated. They were the first among the first territorial regiments to go to France and, apparently, the only one to serve there throughout and well beyond hostilities. Moreover, on 1st November 1914, as 'C' and 'D' squadrons were ordered to drive back or capture 200 Germans who had broken through the line they became the first territorial regiment to come under fire during the Great War.

Disaster at Gallipoli

In 1915, after Russia had appealed for a 'demonstration' against Turkey to relieve pressure in the Caucasus, Lord Kitchener, the Secretary of State for War, asked Winston, as First Lord of the Admiralty, to mount a combined naval and military attack on Constantinople via the Dardanelles. There was, however, considerable indecision about how the proposed attack should be mounted. Lloyd George (Chancellor of the Exchequer) preferred the idea of a move through the Balkans from Greece, with Greek and Rumanian co-operation, which would cut off and destroy the Turkish forces which were assembling in Palestine in order to attack the Suez Canal.

At the beginning of 1915 Kitchener also favoured an attack through the Balkans, but as the Russians (who saw themselves as the true guardians of the Orthodox Church) were strongly opposed to the Greeks getting anywhere near the Holy City of Constantinople, the concept of a combined Balkans operation against Turkey was abandoned.

In the meantime, Kitchener had received an urgent appeal for more troops on the Western Front, and he therefore decided that he could not spare men for a joint naval and military attack on the Dardanelles. On the other hand, he welcomed the idea of a purely naval assault, while Admiral Fisher – now First Sea Lord - was also keen on the idea of using the Navy to force the

Winston as First Lord of the Admiralty.
Hugh Bourn Collection

Dardanelles in order to capture Constantinople and the Gallipoli Peninsula. Winston was, similarly, captivated by the Nelsonic idea of mighty Dreadnought battleships steaming through the Dardanelles while their guns simultaneously destroyed the Turkish forts and batteries on either side of the narrows.

The idea of a full-scale naval attack therefore began to gain momentum although, in the event, the plans were severely compromised when Admiral Fisher decided that the Dreadnoughts would be better employed in an amphibious attack on Schleswig-Holstein. A compromise was therefore reached, whereby an Anglo-French squadron composed largely of pre-Dreadnought battleships would be sent to the Dardanelles under Vice-Admiral Carden, with the brand-new 'super Dreadnought' battleship HMS Queen Elizabeth and the battle-cruiser HMS Inflexible in support. Following a preliminary bombardment in February 1915, the main attack was launched on 18th March – although things had already started to go wrong in that Admiral Carden had suffered a nervous breakdown and had been replaced by his second-in-command, Vice-Admiral de Robeck.

Led by HMS Queen Elizabeth, the Anglo-French fleet was soon in action against the Turkish forts, but it soon became clear that the Turkish gunners were far more skilful than the allies had imagined. HMS Inflexible's bridge was set on fire, while HMS Agamemnon was hit 12 times within half an hour, and a French battleship was holed below the water-line. As the Turkish gunners began to exhaust their supplies of ammunition their fire slackened, and Admiral de Robeck decided to bring up his reserve ships to take the pressure off the elderly French battleships, which had been considerably damaged.

Just after 14.00 hours the French battleship *Suffren* turned to starboard with her three consorts following in a huge arc. Suddenly, the second ship *Bouvet* was shattered by a huge explosion and, in a matter of seconds, she capsized and sank with the loss of around 600 men. The unfortunate ship had already been hit by several heavy shells, and as she was turning under fire it was initially assumed that a 'lucky hit' had penetrated her magazine. About two hours later HMS *Inflexible* struck a mine and began to take in water. This time the cause was clearly understood – the unpleasant truth being underlined just three minutes later when HMS *Irresistible* also reported that she had been mined.

After the loss of three battleships, Admiral de Robeck halted the attack and, ignoring Winston's orders, he refused to renew the action. After further consultation with General Sir Ian Hamilton, who was observing the operation on behalf of Kitchener, the Admiral decided to wait until the army could co-operate.

In reality the Turks had used up most of their ammunition, and if the British had resumed their attack on the following day they would have been virtually unopposed. Although Winston did not know this at the time, he continued to champion the naval operation with undiminished enthusiasm, but with Admiralty opinion rapidly hardening, and with Fisher petulantly demanding the return of HMS *Queen Elizabeth*, the operation was delayed until the army could provide enough troops needed for a combined operation against the Gallipoli Peninsula. In the meantime, the Turks, under their German commander, used the unexpected interval to strengthen their defensive positions. Thus, when the ill-fated attempt to capture Gallipoli by means of amphibious landings commenced on 25th April, the casualties incurred by the British, French, Australian and New Zealand troops in trying to gain a foothold were appalling.

The Gallipoli campaign dragged on until the following October, when the war cabinet decided to evacuate the allied forces from the Dardanelles. The withdrawal, which was completed by January 1916, was conducted with considerable skill and little further loss of life, but the overall campaign had resulted in the loss of 46,000 allied troops, 8,700 of the casualties being Australians while 2,700 were New Zealanders. Although Kitchener and Fisher deserved much of the blame for the disaster, Winston became the principal scapegoat – his shameless egotism, impetuosity and sheer over-confidence having contributed to his downfall.

As a result of Winston's efforts, the QOOH were among the first territorial regiments to see action on the Western Front during World War I. Here, Captain Guy Bonham Carter poses on horseback at Steentje near Bailleul in December 1914. He was to be killed in action, 16th May 1915.

Oxfordshire Yeomanry Trust OXFYT1073

Active Service on the Western Front

The failure at Gallipoli was so serious that it led to the fall of Herbert Asquith's government, the Liberal Prime Minister being forced to form a coalition with the opposition. In return for their support the Tories demanded, somewhat vindictively, the removal of the 'turn-coat' Winston Churchill from the Admiralty, and Winston was thereby forced to accept a less important post as Chancellor of the Duchy of Lancaster – 'a sinecure without duties' which had no relation to the management of the war effort. As the Duke of Marlborough observed in a latter to Winston dated 24th May 1915: 'I gather that you have been flung a bone on which there is little meat'.

On 18th November 1915, following his decision to leave the government, Winston travelled to France to rejoin his Regiment. On arrival at Bologne he was ordered to report to General Sir John French at St. Omer, and after dining with the General, Winston was offered the command of an infantry brigade. It was agreed that, before taking up his duties, he would join a Guards Battalion in order to gain experience of trench warfare.

Le Casque Adrian

It is noticeable from photographs taken at this time that Winston, who loved wearing a variety of different uniforms and headgear, invariably wore the uniform of the Queens Own Oxfordshire Hussars in conjunction with a French 'Adrian' helmet! Although the *casque Adrian* was decidedly non-standard equipment for a British soldier, Winston liked his stylish 'tin hat' so much that, when having his portrait painted by Sir John Lavery, he wore it as an adjunct to his QOOH uniform!

Winston was subsequently offered the command of the 6th Battalion Royal Scots Fusiliers, with the rank of Lieutenant-Colonel – Asquith having vetoed his promotion to brigadier-general. Amusingly, his first campaign was launched the day after his arrival when he announced to the assembled officers, with Churchillian gravitas: *"War is declared, gentlemen - on the lice!"* There was, thereafter, a great deal of work with finger nails and hot irons until the battalion was clear of vermin. He followed this domestic campaign with a shake-up of the offensive against the German trenches on the other side of no-mans land, making the night hideous with fusillades and barrages in an attempt to shatter their nerves. Winston was regarded as a good officer who worked hard at his job and looked after the men in his command. He carried out frequent inspections and insisted on the men taking care of their feet to prevent trench foot. When he led his troops on route marches he ordered them to sing cheerfully, and he inspected the trenches daily, making many improvements.

Although he was stationed in a relatively quiet area of the front Winston often came under fire, and he had a number of narrow escapes from death. On one occasion a dug-out was obliterated by shell fire only seconds after he had left it. It is said that he personally led thirty-eight raids across no-mans-land towards the enemy lines. Desmond Morton, then a young Artillery major, recalled visiting Winston on the front line: 'I went over dead ground to Churchill's HQ. He had a sketching block in his hand, making a drawing of the enemy lines. He was 'doing a Marlborough' calling up fire, demanding help on the flank and turning the whole thing into a major campaign rather than a trench raid to collar a few Germans'.

Winston & the Tanks

Winston's interest in tanks and the development of mechanised warfare had originated during his period of office as First Lord of the Admiralty, when he had argued for the introduction of armoured vehicles with caterpillar tracks, which would be able to cross over trenches and shell craters. In 1915, the 'Land Ships Committee' of the Admiralty was set up, and while he was in still in power at the Admiralty Winston had ordered eighteen tracked 'land ships' at a cost of £70,000. For various reasons, the early trials had come to naught, but in February 1916 Churchill wrote to Clementine recounting ecstatically how his 'caterpillar' had performed extremely well in tests that had been carried out in front of Balfour, the First Lord of the Admiralty. Further 'land ships' were subsequently ordered, and they went into action for the first time at the Battle of the Somme in 1916.

Winston the Gunner

Britain's armed forces were run-down after the 'War to End Wars', one of the many casualties being the Yeomanry which, as a part-time cavalry force unable to be used outside the UK except in cases of dire emergency, seemed to have no future. When the Territorial Army was reformed in 1920 all but 14 of the 53 regiments of Yeomanry were converted to other roles, the Queens Own Oxfordshire Hussars becoming 399 and 400 (QOOHY) Batteries (Worcestershire and Oxfordshire Yeomanry) Brigade, Royal Field Artillery.

Thus, after World War I, in common with many Yeomanry Regiments, the Queens Own Oxfordshire Hussars were converted into an Artillery unit. Despite the fact that the Regiment would continue to be horsed, the change was not at all popular with many of the officers who had served during the Great War. Winston was a notable exception insofar as, having re-enlisted and served as a gunner he attended camp as a Major at Okehampton in 1923.

It has been suggested that the reason for Winston's sudden appearance at Okehampton may have been so that he could qualify for the Territorial Decoration for which, up to that time, he had not done sufficient Territorial Army service. According to Colonel Sir John Thomson, who had joined as a subaltern in 1927, Winston turned up at the camp professing a total ignorance of the technicalities of gunnery. Okehampton Camp is hardly an inviting aspect, particularly in bad weather, and it is established regimental history that Winston – having taken just one look at the camp – immediately booked himself into a convenient inn at the foot of the hill that leads up to the camp. Colonel Thomson says that the regular Royal Artillery adjutant was invited to dine that evening with Winston at the inn in order to teach him the mysteries of gunnery. The lesson is supposed to have been successful that Winston was able to take his Battery out on the very next day and deliver a satisfactory performance.

Winston & the QOOH in World War II

In 1938 Prime Minister Neville Chamberlain doubled the size of the Territorial Army and, as a result, the Oxfordshire Yeomanry became No. 53 Anti-Tank Regiment. Following 'duplication' in the following year the Queens Own Oxfordshire Hussars were re-designated the 63rd (Oxfordshire Yeomanry) Anti-Tank Regiment RA (TA).

The massive expansion of the British army after the withdrawal from Dunkirk was followed by many months of intensive training in order that men who had joined the army 'straight from civilian life' would be ready for battle against the triumphant German armed forces – the eventual liberation of Europe being planned as early as 1940. Much of this training activity took place in Northern Ireland, a part of the world which became very familiar to members of the Oxfordshire Yeomanry and the Oxfordshire & Buckinghamshire Light Infantry - no less than four battalions of the latter regiment being stationed there during the 'middle years' of the war. The Queens Own Oxfordshire Hussars were sent to Northern Ireland under the command of Lieutenant-Colonel John Thomson in June 1940 and, as part of the 61st Division, they were engaged in training and garrison duties.

The formidable build-up of troops in Northern Ireland was considered to be necessary, in great part, because in 1938 Neville Chamberlain had handed over the British bases in Southern Ireland at Berehaven, Queenstown and Lough Swilly to the Dublin government. This action was, needless to say, regarded by Winston as an act of supreme folly verging on treason, as it meant that part of the British Isles would be left virtually undefended in the event of a German invasion. Despite fears of a German attack on Southern Ireland, the *Taoiseach*, Eamon de Valera, was determined that the twenty-six counties would remain strictly neutral, although it should be acknowledged that he increased the size of the Irish army and (more importantly) allowed many thousands of Southern Irishmen to join the British armed forces. At the same time, a secret scheme was devised whereby, in the event of a German landing in Southern Ireland, a formal request for help would be made to Britain and troops would be rushed southwards to help repel the invaders.

Viewed in this light, the presence of the QOOH in Ireland was part of a vitally-important defensive plan, but many members of the Regiment felt that they were not playing a sufficiently important part in the war effort. Steps were therefore taken to get the Queens Own Oxfordshire Hussars transferred away from Ireland to some more active role elsewhere.

Colonel Thomson, who succeeded Winston as Hon. Colonel of the QOOH, believed that the personal intervention of the Prime Minister was decisive in ending the Regiment's somnolent role in Northern Ireland. As a result, half of the Regiment was sent to Malaya as two independent Batteries in 1942. This was shortly before the fall of Singapore when the Queens Own Oxfordshire Hussars contingent were taken into captivity and suffered the experience of the infamous Burma railway. The remainder of the Regiment served in north-western Europe, amalgamated with the Argyll & Sutherland Highlanders, landing after the initial invasion but being the first unit to enter the Bergen-Belsen concentration camp.

Winston & The Queen's Own Oxfordshire Hussars

Winston's term as Honorary Colonel of the Queens Own Oxfordshire Hussars from 1951 until his death in 1965, speaks for itself, as does his selection of an Oxfordshire Yeomanry detachment to march in his Funeral Cortege immediately in front of the mounted Household Cavalry escort. They were, for this reason, the contingent of marching soldiers nearest to his coffin of all the various regiments with which he had been associated in his lifetime.

The foregoing notes seem to demonstrate a level of commitment to 'his' local Yeomanry Regiment that is extraordinary by any standards, even after allowing for Winston's abnormal levels of nervous energy. While his original membership arose by default from his family background, he clearly came to believe that a Yeomanry regiment, raised and handled like the Queens Own Oxfordshire Hussars, was a good way to harness the energies of the enthusiastic amateur. His actions in relation to the Oxfordshire Yeomanry, throughout his long and influential career, strongly suggest that he believed that the Yeomanry in general - and his Yeomanry in particular - had a real and special contribution to make in terms of national defence.

The wartime Prime Minister in the grounds of Ditchley Park, complete with cigar and Homburg hat.

The Ditchley Foundation

Bugle & Sabre Special

POLITICIAN & STATESMAN

Political & Social Connections at Blenheim

Blenheim Palace was a meeting place for various political or quasi-political organisations throughout the late Victorian and Edwardian periods. Many of these functions were associated with the Conservative Party or related organisations such as The Primrose League, while others were of purely local importance, such as flower displays, cricket matches or agricultural shows. Among the more unusual events held at Blenheim was a great review of firemen, which took place in July 1895, while the Oxfordshire Yeomanry camped in Blenheim Park on several occasions, notably in 1901, 1903, 1905, 1906, 1911 and 1912.

Perhaps more importantly, in terms of Winston's social and political connections, great houses such as Blenheim were also the setting for lavish house parties, at which the rich, famous and powerful could meet informally and discuss matters of mutual interest. The Queens Own Oxfordshire Hussars formed part of this social network, insofar as some of the great figures of the day were members of the regiment.

Great Men at 2 Connaught Place

Although Winston undoubtedly met many famous and influential people at Blenheim, he would also have met eminent personalities, both Liberals and Tories, at his father's London houses – No. 2 Connaught Place until 1892, and then 50 Grosvenor Square. Contact with senior political figures such as Arthur Chamberlain, Edward Carson, Arthur Balfour, Herbert Asquith and Lord Rosebery must have been a source of interest and inspiration for the young Winston.

The Member for Oldham

Oldham is an industrial town in South-Eastern Lancashire. Its economy was traditionally based upon the manufacture of fustian, and as the Industrial Revolution gathered momentum Oldham rapidly became a noted centre of the cotton-spinning industry. By 1825 there were 65 mills in the Oldham area, many of these being water-driven, although other mills were already powered by steam engines.

Further mechanisation of the textile industry during the early 19th century resulted in the appearance of large multi-storied spinning mills, while the success of the cotton-spinning industry resulted in a huge increase in Oldham's population from 5,200 in 1801 to 96,000 in 1901, and 147,483 by 1921. There were, by 1913, around 19 million cotton spindles in operation within four miles of the town hall, Oldham's cotton-spinning capacity being 'rather larger than the combined cotton-spinning strength of all France and Germany'.

It is at first glance hard to see why, in 1899, Winston should have been nominated as a Conservative candidate for this archetypal mill town, although, in reality, many of the Lancashire industrial towns were strongly Tory in sentiment. This may be a legacy of the 1830s, when local Tories had been strongly opposed to the introduction of workhouses under the provisions of the New Poor Law. At the same time, many of the Lancashire gentry were Tories – their influence being such that significant numbers of mill workers were happy to vote for what they regarded as the party of church, state and Empire. It seemed, therefore, that by standing for election as a Tory candidate in the summer of 1899 Winston would have every chance of success.

Oldham was, in those days, a two-member constituency, and there were two Liberal and two Conservative candidates – the other Tory, apart from Winston, being Mr James Mawdsley, the General Secretary of the Lancashire Branch of the Amalgamated Society of Cotton Spinners. Unfortunately, Messrs Churchill & Mawdsley were standing against two excellent Liberal candidates – Walter Runciman, a member of a wealthy ship-owning family, and Albert Emmott, a popular local mill-owner. The results, as declared on 6th July 1899, were as follows:

Emmott (Radical) .... 12,976 votes
Runciman (Radical) .... 12,770 votes
Churchill (Conservative) .... 11,477 votes
Mawdsley (Conservative) .... 11,449 votes

A little over one year later, in July 1900, Winston returned from South Africa as a war hero, and when he visited Oldham he received what he described in a latter to his brother as an extraordinary reception: *"Over 10,000 people turned out in the streets with flags and drums beating and shouted themselves hoarse for two hours, and although it was 12 o'clock before I left the Conservative Club, the streets were still crowded with people. I don't think the two radical members are at all pleased with the idea of me standing against them"*. Having been re-adopted as a Conservative candidate, Winston was elected after a short campaign, the results as declared shortly before midnight on 1st October 1900 being:

Emmott (Radical) .... 12,947 votes
Churchill (Conservative) .... 12,931 votes
Runciman (Radical) .... 12,709 votes
Crisp (Conservative) .... 12,522 votes

A Change of Party

It has been said, with considerable justification, that Winston Churchill was never a party politician. This was made abundantly clear in his very first speech in Parliament, when he criticised his own government and took the side of the recently-defeated Boers:

*"If I were a Boer fighting in the field – and if I were a Boer, I hope I **should** be fighting in the field – I should not allow*

myself to be taken in by any message of sympathy …. I have often myself been very much ashamed to see respectable old Boer farmers – the Boer is a curious combination of the squire and the peasant, and under the rough coat of the peasant there are very often to be found the instincts of a squire – I have been ashamed to see such men ordered about by young subaltern officers as if they were private soldiers".

Soon, he was urging the adoption of Gladstone's old slogan 'Peace, Retrenchment and Reform' as a Tory motto, and this brought him into direct conflict with his colleague Joseph Chamberlain (1836-1914), who was advocating an alternative policy of trade protection and Imperial Preference. When the Tories adopted Chamberlain's protectionist policies, Winston crossed the floor of the House, and on 31st May 1904 he took his seat beside David Lloyd George on the Liberal benches.

Member for North-West Manchester

As a result of his dramatic defection to the Liberals, Winston was disowned by the Oldham Conservative Association but, having stood as a Liberal candidate for North-West Manchester in the 1906 General Election, he won this formerly-Tory seat with a respectable majority of 1,241. The campaign was marked by an alarming incident when, at a meeting held in a covered-over public swimming bath, the temporary wooden floor gave way and plunged the audience into the empty bath. Seizing the moment, Winston cried out *"let justice be done, even though the floor falls in!"*, and the impending panic dissolved into a roar of laughter.

Although he was a very recent a recruit to the Liberal ranks, Winston had already made such a favourable impression that office was found for him in the new Government as Under-Secretary for the Colonies. This new role had a particular advantage in that the Secretary, Lord Elgin, was a member of the Upper House, and Winston thereby became responsible for explaining and defending the Government's colonial policies in the House of Commons.

Although he undoubtedly relished his work as an MP, Winston was well aware that party politics could be a ruthless and dirty business, and in a letter to Pamela Plowden he commented that: *"In politics one needs to have bowls of chilled India rubber. All sorts of influences from the gentlest and the kindest to the most cruel and slanderous are employed to weaken an attack. But I am gradually becoming proof against everything".*

Winston & The Kaiser

It could be argued that the Churchill family knew Kaiser Wilhelm II socially, for on Friday 24th November 1899 the German Emperor had been conveyed by special train from Windsor to Blenheim & Woodstock so that he could attend a luncheon party at Blenheim Palace – the journey from Windsor to Woodstock being accomplished in 1 hour 15 minutes. Although Winston was in South Africa at the time of the Kaiser's visit, the Emperor was well aware of his political and social connections.

In September 1906 Winston, in his new role as Under-Secretary to the Colonies, was invited to Germany as a guest of the German army at the 'Kaisermanoeuvre', which was to be held at Breslau in Silesia. The German Emperor obviously regarded Winston as a rising politician and person of influence, and he was treated as an honoured guest.

In addition to attending spectacular mock battles and lavish full-dress banquets, he had several serious and confidential talks with the Kaiser about Africa and other matters of mutual interest. However, prior to his departure from England, the King had sent Winston a clear message via the Prime Minister, warning him about being 'too communicative and frank with his nephew'. It is interesting to note that, in photographs taken at the 1906 Kaisermanoeuvre, Winston is clearly wearing his uniform as a major in the Queens Own Oxfordshire Hussars.

Winston much admired the obvious skills and discipline of the German troops, but he wondered *"how they would stand up to musketry"*. In a letter to Lord Elgin, the Colonial Secretary, he said: *"I do not think they have appreciated the terrible power of the weapons they hold and modern fire conditions, and have in that and in minor respects much to learn from our army, yet numbers, quality, discipline and organisation are four good roads to victory"*. The manoeuvres were, in effect, a piece of grand theatre, carefully choreographed and involving thousands of participants densely packed into massed formations that reminded Winston of the great charge of the Dervishes at Omdurman.

Kaiser Wilhelm, wrote Winston, *"was then at the height of his glory"*. He rode *"his magnificent horse at the head of a squadron of cuirassiers, wearing their white uniform and eagle-crested helmet"*. He sat on his horse *"surrounded by Kings and Princes while his legions defiled before him in what seemed to be an endless procession"*. Then came a glorious parade of *"German military and Imperial splendour so brilliantly displayed to foreign eyes"*, but the fifty thousand troops, *"avalanches of field guns"* and *"squadrons of motor cars"* that passed in review before the Kaiser for more than five hours represented, as Winston recorded *"only a twentieth of the armed strength of the regular German Army before mobilization"*.

"This Army is a Terrible Engine"

In 1909, Winston was again invited by the Kaiser to observe the German Army Manoeuvres which, on this occasion, were held at Wurzburg. Whereas the earlier manoeuvres had been a great and colourful pageant, in 1909 the huge German army presented a much more menacing appearance to foreign observers. In a revealing letter to his wife Clementine, he wrote: *"This army is a terrible engine. It marches sometimes 35 miles a day. It is in number as the sands of the sea – and with all the modern conveniences"*.

The deployments and equipment were much more practical than the glittering cohorts of 1906, and far more up-to-date in their tactics. The large masses of infantry seen previously – which so would so easily have been

As a high-ranking member of Asquith's Liberal government, Churchill was a supporter of the Irish Home Rule Bill, and it must have caused him considerable embarrassment when, on 27th July 1912, his ancestral home at Blenheim became the setting for an enormous anti-Home Rule 'demonstration' – over 20,000 Unionists being conveyed to Blenheim & Woodstock station by special trains from London, Shrewsbury, Norwich, the Midlands and the North of England. The speakers included Winston's close friend F. E. Smith, together with Edward Carson and Bonar Law, who expressed their full support for whatever action Irish Unionists might take in their fight to remain full British citizens.

Oxfordshire Yeomanry Trust OXYT128

wiped out by modern artillery and machine guns – had vanished, while the artillery was no longer positioned in long lines, as though on a parade ground, but placed where they would be tactically advantageous. As Winston reported, with typical perspicacity:

"The manoeuvres at Wurzburg showed a great change in German military tactics. A remarkable stride had been made in modernizing their infantry formations and adapting them to actual war conditions. The absurdities of the Silesian manoeuvres were not repeated. The dense masses were rarely, if ever, seen. The Artillery was not ranged in long lines, but dotted about wherever conveniences of the ground suggested. The whole extent of the battlefield was far greater. The Cavalry were hardly at all in evidence, and then only on distant flanks. The Infantry advanced in successive skirmishing lines, and machine-guns everywhere had begun to be a feature. Although their formations were still to British eyes much too dense for modern fire, they nevertheless constituted an enormous advance upon 1906".

Friendship with David Lloyd George

Winston's friendship with David Lloyd George (1863-1945) was one of the most important formative influences on his political career. It began when Winston made his Maiden Speech in the House of Commons, attacking Lloyd George – who had cut short his own speech in order to make way for him. The friendship lasted for over forty years, whether they were political allies or opponents.

The two men came from markedly different backgrounds, Winston being a member of the aristocracy with a public school education, whereas Lloyd George had been brought up by a cobbler uncle in a remote Welsh village and received his education at a National school. Yet, at the same time, these two politicians had very much in common - they were both rebellious, highly-energetic and flamboyant showmen with a flair for oratory and a passion for social justice, and they were (and still are) highly-controversial figures, who will be remembered as the two great British war leaders of the 20th century.

Lloyd George, then serving as President of the Board of Trade, had introduced a range of reforming legislation including the Merchant Shipping Act, the Patents Act, and the securing of better conditions for railwaymen. Following the example of his father, Winston had entered politics as a Tory radical with an interest in social reform, but the influence of Lloyd George can perhaps be detected in his speech on the evils of unemployment, which was made in February 1908:

"In my opinion, the question of unemployment is the greatest of the day. The people never complain without terrible cause, and we have to solve the question of the crying need of a man who finds himself unable to get employment. I am not one of those who say that everybody should be equal, but what I do say is that no one should have anything unless everybody has something. The general trend of Liberal policy must be increasingly to build up the minimum standards of life and labour in this country".

In the years that followed, Winston and Lloyd George became the two really outstanding figures in British politics. Lloyd George was, at first, the senior partner, but as Winston grew in political stature he became the equal of his older mentor. Hostile critics tried to hint at rivalries and jealousies between the two great men, but in reality their friendship was too firm and genuine for any such rivalries to spring up. When in 1915 Winston was forced to resign as a result of the Gallipoli disaster, Lloyd George was bereft, and Lord Riddell commented: 'Like a political Mrs Gummidge, he still hankers after Winston'.

Member for Dundee

In 1908 Winston lost his North West Manchester seat to the delight of the Tories. A few days earlier, he had been entirely confident that the more unpredictable elements in the voting population, such as the Jews, the Irish and the Free Traders, would vote in his favour. But, following a 6.6 per cent swing against him, he blamed his defeat on *"sulky Irish Catholics"*. Although he had lost his seat, Winston was now so highly regarded by the Liberal Party that he was offered the ultra-safe Liberal seat of Dundee. He was duly elected on 9th May 1908 and, at the age of 33, he entered the Cabinet, not as First Lord of the Admiralty (the post which Asquith had first suggested to him) but as Lloyd George's successor at the Board of Trade.

Winston & The Fabians

Winston's social policies were considerable influenced by the Fabian socialists, Sidney and Beatrice Webb. They took lunch with Winston and Clementine Churchill on 10th October 1908, and Beatrice commented that Clementine was 'a charming lady, well-bred and pretty and earnest with it, but not rich, by no means a 'good match', which is to Winston's credit'. She compared Winston favourably with Lloyd George, and was pleased that he 'had made a really eloquent speech on the unemployed the night before'.

Although Winston could never be described as a socialist, he had clearly been aware of the problems experienced by working class people in his own constituencies of Oldham, Manchester and Dundee. He also studied the social surveys carried out by Seebohm Rowntree and Charles Booth and, following the example of Lloyd George, he started to introduce social reform Bills into Parliament, resulting in Acts to regulate working conditions in the mines; a Trade Boards Bill that prohibited sweated labour; unemployment insurance; and the creation of national Labour Exchanges.

The Siege of Sidney Street

Notwithstanding Winston's growing interest in social policy, he retained a lively appetite for action and adventure, which came into full play on 3rd January 1911 when a gang of Russian anarchists led by 'Peter the Painter' killed three policemen in a botched jewel robbery and then took refuge in a house in Sidney Street, off the Mile End Road. After they had callously shot down another policeman, Winston, now serving as Home Secretary, sent for a platoon of Scots Guards from the Tower of London to reinforce the armed police cordon around the barricaded house.

Winston, wearing his top-hat and a fine astrakhan-collared overcoat, turned up to direct the siege and, following three more police casualties, the besieged building caught fire. The fire brigade hurried to the scene, but Winston used his authority to prevent the firemen from exercising their statutory duty to extinguish any fires in the Metropolitan area. He had, in the interim, ordered up the artillery to ensure the total destruction of the house and those inside it.

The anarchists were left with two choices – they could be shot dead when they emerged into the street, or burn to death. Eventually two charred corpses were found in the ruins, although it is thought that 'Peter the Painter' somehow managed to escape. The 'Siege of Sidney Street' provided a field day for the press and for Churchill's many Tory critics, who considered that his conduct had been in some way unseemly for a Home Secretary. Winston, however, was so excited by the siege that his incipient lisp became much worse than usual, and when reproached by his Secretary at the Home Office he said 'Now Charleth, don't be croth, it woth such fun'.

Bugle & Sabre Special

Winston served as Chancellor of the Exchequer from 1924 until 1929.   *Hugh Bourn Collection*

In the Wilderness

Winston, suffering from appendicitis, was defeated as a Liberal in the 1922 General Election, but in 1924 he was re-elected as the 'Constitutionalist' MP for Epping. Events were now driving him back into the Tory Party. He served as the Member for Epping throughout the Depression years of the 1930s, but he was never entirely happy with Stanley Baldwin, Neville Chamberlain or his other lacklustre Conservative colleagues.

After several years in the political wilderness – in which time he had spoken out against the appeasement of foreign dictators – Winston was appointed Prime Minister on 10th May 1940. The Liberal and Labour parties, who had refused to serve under Neville Chamberlain, immediately accepted Winston's invitation to join a Coalition Government. Two days later, he announced the formation of an Inner War Cabinet of just five members.

Winston & Ditchley Park

As wartime Prime Minister, it might be thought that Winston would have spent little time in Oxfordshire but, in reality, this was not in fact the case. In the early part of the war it was considered that the Prime Minister's official country residence at Chequers was too conspicuous at full moon and might be a prestigious target for the Luftwaffe. While not wishing to evade the dangers being experienced by the population at large, Winston accepted the extreme vulnerability of Chequers and he told Clement Attlee, his Deputy Prime Minister, that 'whilst he did not object to chance, he felt it would be a mistake to be the victim of design'.

Meanwhile, Ronald Tree MP, had offered the Prime Minister the use of his 18th century country house at Ditchley Park, near Oxford, which was closely surrounded by a park of mature trees and was much less conspicuous from the air. Winston first went to Ditchley in lieu of Chequers on 9th November 1940, accompanied by Clementine and his daughter Mary. Winston was already familiar with the house (and the quality of its cellar) since he and Clementine had been guests in 1937, when Ronald Tree was one of the small group of MPs who had shared his concern about the growing Nazi menace. Ronald Tree and his wife Nancy were American by birth but had Anglo-American citizenship. Ronald had been MP for the Harborough division of Leicestershire since 1933 and, having been personal private secretary to Sir John Reith and Alfred Duff Cooper, he was then working as Private Secretary to Winston's protégé, Brendan Bracken. He had acquired Ditchley Park in 1933 after the death of the 17th Viscount Dillon.

Ditchley had been the home of the Dillon and Lee families for over 300 years and, as such, it could claim to be the ancestral home of Robert E. Lee, the Confederate general. When Ronald Tree bought it he described it as presenting 'an unforgettable picture of magnificence and accumulated junk', but by 1940 the junk had been cleared and the magnificence restored. For Winston's first visit special telephone lines, with a scrambling system, were installed. Accommodation was provided for the Prime Minister's advisory staff and secretariat, as well as billets for a full company of the Oxfordshire & Buckinghamshire Light Infantry who would guard the house. To Ronald Tree's relief, when Winston left on the following Monday he said that he had been very satisfied and would be back the following weekend, 'high moon or no high moon!'.

Winston had, in fact, just left Downing Street for Ditchley Park the following weekend when he opened a top secret message which had been handed to him as he was getting into the car, and told the driver to turn back. An Enigma decrypt indicated the prospect of a massive air raid on London, and Winston said that he was not going to spend the night 'peacefully in the country while the metropolis was under heavy attack'. In the event, over four hundred German bombers that night attacked Coventry, thirty miles from Ditchley. Winston returned

Bugle & Sabre Special

Winston watches an artillery barrage from an observation post in the Italian hills near Florence during World War II. The senior officer standing at his rear is thought to be Brigadier Julian St. Clair Holbrook CBE MC, commanding No. 6 Army Group Royal Artillery. This oil-on-canvas painting is signed 'Webb'.

Hugh Bourn Collection

to Ditchley at regular intervals over the next two years. The last weekend occasion being on 26th September 1942, when he was again accompanied by Clementine and Mary. It happened to be Ronald Tree's birthday, the United States had now entered the war and Churchill was in high good spirits. Winston's last visit to Ditchley, for lunch, was in March 1943.

Winston's Favourite Film

If Winston was spending the weekend at Chequers or Ditchley Park the guests were often invited to join him in watching a film. His favourite film, produced in Hollywood by his friend Alexander Korda, was *Lady Hamilton* (1941) starring Laurence Olivier as Admiral Lord Nelson and Vivien Leigh in the title role as Lady Hamilton. By this time, writes Paul Addison, 'it would be nearly midnight, and Winston was ready to return to work. Struggling to keep their eyes open, his advisers would be summoned to meetings at which key strategic or operational issues were being discussed and informal decisions reached. Winston's midnight follies, as they were known in Whitehall, caused much resentment among the exhausted officials who were compelled to attend them. Often Churchill would work until three or four in the morning before taking his sleeping capsules and retiring to bed'.

Winston & The Secret Services

Despite his military background, Winston did not entirely trust the regular army. He felt more at home in the company of unconventional military figures, and had a particular affinity with those whom he regarded as 'gifted amateurs'. It is, perhaps, hardly surprising that, in 1909, he should have advocated the creation of a Secret Service Bureau. In the following year, this new organisation was divided into separate 'Home' and 'Foreign' departments – the predecessors of MI5 and MI6 respectively. As Home Secretary, Winston would obviously have been intimately connected with these developments, which had considerable success in combating German 'spy rings' at the start of World War I.

Winston and the SOE

In World War II, Winston was an enthusiastic supporter of 'SOE', the 'Special Operations Executive' – a secret army of British agents who risked their lives by going undercover in France and other occupied countries. The origins of SOE can probably be traced to a meeting held at the Foreign Office on 1st July 1940, as a result of which Hugh Dalton, Winston's 'Minster of Economic Warfare', set out the aims of the proposed 'secret army' as follows:

"We have got to organize movements in enemy-occupied territory comparable to the Sinn Fein movement in Ireland, to the Chinese Guerillas now operating against Japan, to the Spanish Irregulars who played a notable part in Wellington's campaign or - one might as well admit it – to the organizations which the Nazis

A wood-carving commemorating Winston's famous 'We Will Never Surrender' speech, which was made to the House of Commons on 4th June 1940. *Hugh Bourn Collection*

themselves have developed so remarkably in almost every country in the world. This 'democratic international' must use many different methods, including industrial and military sabotage, labour agitation and strikes, continuous propaganda, terrorist acts against traitors and German leaders, boycotts and riots.

It is quite clear to me that an organization on this scale and of this character is not something which can be handled by the ordinary departmental machinery of either the British Civil Service or the British military machine. What is needed is a new organization to co-orainate, inspire, control and assist the nationals of the oppressed countries who must themselves be the

Bugle & Sabre Special

Two views showing Winston inspecting the guard at Ditchley Park during World War Two. The troops visible in the upper view being members of the Free Czech forces, while those in the lower photograph are members of the Oxfordshire & Buckinghamshire Light Infantry.
The Ditchley Foundation

A further glimpse of Winston inspecting the troops at Ditchley Park. It is believed that the guard was provided, on this occasion, by a company of the Oxfordshire & Buckinghamshire Light Infantry. *The Ditchley Foundation*

direct participants. We need absolute secrecy, a certain fanatical enthusiasm, willingness to work with people of different nationalities, complete political reliability. Some of these qualities are certainly to be found in some military officers and, if such men are available, they should undoubtedly be used. But the organization should, in my view, be entirely independent of the War Office machine".

These aims and aspirations were music to Winston's ears, and on 16th July 1940 he asked Dalton to take ministerial charge of the new organisation, with the memorable instruction 'set Europe ablaze'. In similar vein, Winston suggested that SOE, which initially operated under the cover of the Ministry of Economic Warfare, should become 'The Ministry of Ungentlemanly Warfare'! Winston also took a great interest in the work of the SOE explosives & 'devices' section, which was located at 35 Portland Place, in London, until the Autumn of 1940, when it moved to a country house known as 'The Firs', near Aylesbury (later 'Station MD1'), where 'devices' such as pressure switches and exploding rats could be tested in greater secrecy.

James Bond

The Queens Own Oxfordshire Hussars have a link with the fictional 'James Bond' character, insofar as Valentine Fleming, the father of novelist Ian Fleming, served in the Regiment alongside Winston and F. E. Smith. Ian Fleming worked in naval intelligence during World War II, while his brother Peter was associated with SOE. In this way, real-life experiences provided an inspiration for the James Bond novels – an obvious example being the spy-master 'M', who is generally believed to have been based upon William Melville (1850-1918) – the Irish policeman who became Winston's real-life spy-master in the years before World War I.

The wartime Prime Minister in a characteristic pose.
Hugh Bourn Collection

Bugle & Sabre Special

A Queens Own Oxfordshire Hussars officer's tunic.
Oxfordshire Yeomanry Trust OXFYT519

A Queens Own Oxfordshire Hussars officer's sabretache badge.
Oxfordshire Yeomanry Trust OXFYT180

A QOOH undress sabretache badge. The regimental badge, which was first worn in 1835, depicts the entwined initials of Queen Adelaide.
Oxfordshire Yeomanry Trust OXFYT980

A pair of Queens Own Oxfordshire Hussars collar badges also incorporating the 'AR' cipher.
Oxfordshire Yeomanry Trust OXFYT1056

A Primrose League medallion awarded for 'special service' during the 1900 General Election. The Primrose League was formed in 1883 with the aim of promoting Tory principles – the primrose being Benjamin Disraeli's favourite flower. By 1900 the League had about one and a half million members. The Latin motto IMPERIUM ET LIBERTAS means 'Empire & Liberty'.
Hugh Bourn Collection

HIGH SOCIETY

A Perfect Gentleman

Although Winston was essentially a romantic, who had many close female friends, he appears to have behaved as a perfect gentleman in terms of romantic attachments. Indeed, compared with many members of his racy, aristocratic circle, he was decidedly puritanical in his relationships – Winston Churchill was never a philanderer, and no trace of scandal ever sullied his name.

Winston's Lost Love

Winston suffered heartbreak when his hopes of marrying Pamela Plowden (1873-1971), the first great love of his life were dashed by his lack of money and any immediate prospects of success. Churchill had fallen in love at first sight with Pamela when they had met at a polo match at Secunderabad, some ten miles from Hyderabad in November 1896. He wrote to his mother: *"I was introduced yesterday to Miss Pamela Plowden – who lives here. I must say that she is the most beautiful girl I have ever seen – bar none, as the Duchess Lily says. We are going to try and do the City of Hyderabad together – on an elephant. You dare not walk or natives spit at Europeans – which provokes retaliation leading to riots"*. The visit to Hyderabad having been a success, Winston dined with the Plowdens, and on 12th November 1896 he wrote to his mother, telling her that Pamela was *"very beautiful and clever"*.

Pamela, a renowned society beauty, was a few months older than Winston. She was the daughter of Sir Trevor Chichele-Plowden, at that time the British Resident in Hyderabad. She was the first significant love of Churchill's life, and it appears that the love was reciprocated. Winston's mother, Lady Randolph Churchill, wrote to him before his return from South Africa to say that: 'Pamela is devoted to you and if your love has grown as hers – I have no doubt it is only a question of time for you two to marry'.

Churchill proposed to Pamela Plowden when he was in his early twenties, and it is thought that they were informally engaged. But just two years later she married Victor, then 2nd Earl of Lytton (1876-1947), the son of a Viceroy of India. A letter released by Pamela's descendants shows Churchill was acutely aware that his financial situation was a bar to marriage. Writing from Calcutta in March 1899, he began *"My dear Miss Pamela"* and told her: *"I have lived all my life seeing the most beautiful women London produces… Never have I seen one for whom I would forego the business of life. Then I met you… Were I a dreamer of dreams, I would say… 'Marry me – and I will conquer the world and lay it at your feet'. For marriage two conditions are necessary – money and the consent of both parties. One certainly, both probably are absent. And this is all such an old story"*.

A colour-tinted photograph showing Winston as Under Secretary for the Colonies, circa 1908.

Hugh Bourn Collection

'Everything seemed to be Purely Platonic'

In December 1900 Winston spent Christmas as the guest of Lord and Lady Minto in Government House in Ottawa. Pamela was also present and, in a letter to his mother, Winston wrote that *"Pamela was there, very pretty and quite happy. We had no painful discussions, but there is no doubt in my mind that she is the only woman I could ever live happily with"*. Lord Minto, in reporting back to Lady Randolph, suggested that 'everything seemed to me to be entirely platonic – but I am becoming so humdrum that it is difficult for me to imagine that anyone ever had any other feelings than those of Plato'.

In 1902 Winston wrote to the Earl of Lytton, graciously congratulating him on his engagement to Pamela, and wishing them *"all the happiness & good fortune which wit & beauty deserve when they combine to share the inheritance of the future"*, and trusting he would always be counted *"among your most devoted friends"*. Winston nevertheless remained a close friend of Pamela and, some six years later, he sent her a letter marked 'Secret till Sat[urda]y', announcing his forthcoming marriage to Clementine Hosier.

When Pamela's husband died in October 1947 Winston wrote the following letter from his home at Chartwell, the sentiments being typically Churchillian:

"I am deeply grieved at Victor's death and at your own sorrow. I had no idea that he was so ill until saw in the papers of Saturday an alarming report - and now he is gone. A life of great ability, of high ideals, of distinguished gifts has come to its end. At seventy and over we have reached our allotted span and death cannot be regarded as a foe. More especially in this time when so much in our present existence is shattered and lies dark among the ruins of the once glittering structures of our youth. Victor leaves an already honoured name with a new and mellow light around it. What fearful blows you bore together when all your hopes were cut down! What happiness Victor must have gained from his long life with you! Any now darling Pamela you are all alone in this bleak and darkening world but I am sure your gleaming spirit will shine thus brighter in the gathering gloom. I do hope to see you soon. You are so much in my thoughts and perhaps a talk might be a comfort. Perhaps you will let me know".

Winston's First Meeting with Clementine Hozier

Winston first met Clementine Hozier (1885-1977), his future wife, at a fashionable London ball in the summer of 1904, when he was twenty-nine. Clementine was the second child of Colonel Sir Henry Hozier and Lady Blanche (nee Ogilvy), and the grand daughter of the Countess of Airlie – an influential figure in Winston's constituency of Dundee. Her father, Colonel Hozier of the 3rd Dragoon Guards, was a soldier, military attaché, author and Secretary to the Corporation of Lloyds of London. Clementine had had two very close admirers, to both of whom she had been engaged. One of these was Lionel Earle, a wealthy civil servant, who was many years older than Clementine, while the other was the Honourable Sidney Peel, the grandson of Prime Minister Sir Robert Peel and an officer in the Queens Own Oxfordshire Hussars.

Proposal of Marriage at Blenheim

In April 1908 Churchill was re-introduced to Clementine at a dinner party given by Lady St Helier. According to Winston's friend Violet Asquith, she had a 'face of classical perfection ... a profile like the prow of a Greek ship'. Winston and Clementine began to correspond, and in the following August 1908, their friendship having deepened, she agreed to visit Blenheim Palace as part of a house party that included Lady Randolph, F. E. Smith and many of Winston's closest friends. Winston had written a letter of invitation to Clementine, encouraging her to come and describing the pleasures of Blenheim Palace – its rose gardens, pools, lakes and gardens. On 11th August the couple were caught in a shower of rain while walking in the grounds, and they took refuge in the Temple of Diana, overlooking the Great Lake. There, Winston proposed to Clementine, and was accepted.

Marriage to Clementine

The wedding of Winston and Clementine took place on 15th August 1908 at St. Margaret's Church, Westminster, the parish church of the house of commons. Bishop Edwards

Clementine Churchill. *The Lady Soames*

of St. Asaph officiated, Dean Welldon of Manchester (Winston's headmaster at Harrow) gave the address, Lord Hugh Cecil was best man and David Lloyd George signed the register, while huge crowds turned out to wish them well. Curiously, and somewhat unfairly, *The Tailor and Cutter* thought that Winston's wedding garments gave him the appearance of 'a sort of glorified coachman' – a reference, perhaps, to the shape of his top hat – although the wedding photographs suggest that all of the gentlemen at the wedding sported similar frock-coats and top hats. The bride wore diamond earrings and a lustrous white satin gown, with a flowing veil of soft tulle. She was given away by her brother Bill Hozier. After a honeymoon in Italy the newly-married couple set up home in Churchill's refurbished bachelor flat in Bolton Street.

"I Married & Lived Happily Ever Afterwards"

In his book *My Early Life*, written some twenty-two years later, Winston stated simply but sincerely *"I married and lived happily ever afterwards"*, and his closest friends agreed that this statement was demonstrably true. Winston and

A photograph of Clementine Churchill dated 25th April 1925
Hugh Bourn Collection

Clementine remained devoted to each other for the rest of their married life, their affection being expressed by the use of pet names – Winston being known as 'Pig' or 'Pug', while Clementine was 'Kat'; the children, when they started to arrive, were referred-to as 'the Kittens'.

In the words of Malcolm Thompson: 'Their loyalty left no room for the intrusion of rivals. Mrs Churchill's poised personality was to prove the ideal complement to Winston's impulsive restlessness. As wife and mother, as hostess and companion, building for him a happy home life, and fostering his friendships and social contacts, sharing his joys and sorrows, his disappointments and successes, her shining example stands. If Winston Churchill well served his country and his age, she can claim share in the credit'.

Winston's Friendship with Violet Asquith

It has been suggested that the women in Winston's life could be divided into two distinct categories 'the virginal snowdrops, unsullied by experience, or even knowledge, of the seamy side of life', and the more forceful, confident 'women of the world', some of whom became his close friends. Pamela Plowden and Clementine Hosier fell into the former category, whereas Violet Asquith (1887-1969), who later became Lady Violet Bonham Carter was perhaps an example of the latter. The only daughter of Herbert Asquith, Violet was denied an academic education, but she nevertheless developed a deep knowledge of contemporary politics which made here 'one of the most outstanding women of her generation'.

On one notable occasion, Violet persuaded Winston to go to Aberdeenshire where he 'flung himself with zest into our favourite and most perilous pastime of rock-climbing, revelling in the scramble up crags and cliffs, the precarious transition from ledge to ledge, with slippery sea-weed underfoot and roaring seas below .... He always took command of every operation, decreeing strategy and tactics and even dictating the correct position of our arms and legs. He brought to every ploy the excitement of a child and, like a child, he made it seem not only exciting but serious and important'.

Voyages Aboard HMY Enchantress

In November 1911 Prime Minster Herbert Asquith offered Winston the post of First Lord of the Admiralty, and during the first three peacetime years of his tenure he spent no less than eight months aboard the Admiralty steam yacht *Enchantress* – use of this luxurious yacht being an official perquisite of the First Lord and members of the Admiralty Board. Built at Belfast in 1903, the *Enchantress* was a handsome vessel with a raked, clipper bow. She had a crew of nearly 200, and was ideal for visiting dockyards, ports and harbours throughout the world. The Asquiths and their friends were frequent guests, and Violet Asquith recalled 'The memory of those golden journeys in our enchanted ship' which could never fade.

In May 1913, for example, Winston and Clementine accompanied Herbert Asquith, his wife Margot, Violet Asquith, Edward Marsh and Masterton-Smith on an idyllic, three-week Whitson cruise from Venice to Dalmatia, Greece and Malta – the voyage being a welcome holiday for the Prime Minister, who was able to play bridge, read extensively and indulge his interest in classical scholarship. Writing while cruising off the coast of Albania, Asquith wrote:

"As you can imagine, it is a journey which affords endless opportunities for the conscientious student of Baedeker, and after nearly a week's experience I can assure you that you need not fear the rivalry of any of my present trip-fellows. Eddie and Masterton are both good at the Classical side, but neither of them has any notion of the unimportant things which it is right and fruitful to remember. Winston is, of course, quite hopeless: his most salient remark as we wandered through Diocletian's Palace at Spolato was: 'I should like to bombard the swine'. Margot and Violet, as you know, do not excel in this branch of research, and Clemmie is very patchy".

Confined aboard the *Enchantress* with Winston, Asquith observed his colleague with a mixture of admiration and amusement. By chance, an international incident was being played out at Scutari, and in the same letter from Albania, the Prime Minister wrote: 'It was with great difficulty that I prevented Winston from going himself to Scutari to witness (if not preside over) the surrender of the town. I did not want another Sidney Street in Albania'. Later, when the *Enchantress* reached Malta he reported: 'Winston never set foot on shore at Syracuse, but dictated in his cabin a treatise (which I am about to read) on the world's supplies of oil'.

Yeomanry Camps

It was in may ways typical of the contradictions in Winston's character that, having criticised the Germans for presenting a glittering, but essentially old-fashioned display of cavalry at the 1906 Kaisermanoeuvre, he should have revelled in a similar pageant when it formed part of an Oxfordshire Yeomanry summer camp. In 1911, the Annual Queens Own Oxfordshire Hussars summer camp was held at Blenheim between 25th May and 6th June. On this occasion, the Oxfordshire Yeomanry were brigaded with the Buckinghamshire Yeomanry. Often the squadrons would gallop over the Downs or have a Field Day against the Berkshire Yeomanry, and Churchill described to Clementine how he and his brother 'Jack' had led the squadrons at a furious pace, to the applause of the crowd, while the Berkshires struggled to keep up. According to Churchill, he had made the commanding general order the entire brigade – some 1,200 men and horses - to gallop the length of Blenheim Park in a 'brigade mass', an exercise that he thought had gone 'awfully well'.

Winston & F. E. Smith

Sir Frederick Edwin Smith (later Lord Birkenhead) was perhaps one of Churchill's greatest friends. In the House of Commons in 1906 'FE', as he was generally known, was a brilliant orator, a legal genius, a Conservative MP, Solicitor-General, Lord Chancellor and Secretary of State for India. Winston and 'FE' were, on occasions, political opponents – notably during the Ulster crisis of 1912 when 'FE', Edward Carson and Bonar Law had bitterly opposed the Irish Home Rule Bill, which would have placed the predominantly Protestant counties of north-eastern Ireland under the control of a Catholic-dominated Irish Parliament in Dublin. Clementine, who disliked 'FE', thought he was coarse, a drinker, a gambler and a bad influence on her husband, though she did allow him to become Randolph's godfather. Clementine was also friendly with his wife Margaret.

F. E. Smith in the Glass-House

In January 1916 when F. E. Smith was attending a conference in Paris in company with Bonar Law and David Lloyd George, he decided to pay a visit to the front lines in order to see what Winston was doing. This led to an amusing incident when the Army GHQ refused to issue the necessary permit for a visit the Front. Undeterred, 'FE' decided to visit Winston without the necessary pass and, in consequence, the Provost-Marshal ordered his arrest. He was dragged out of bed at Winston's dug-out, and carted off ignominiously to GHQ, where he was placed

Winston's close friend Frederick Edward ('FE') Smith (1872-1930), the first Lord Birkenhead, rose from comparatively humble beginnings to become Lord Chancellor of England. Having entered politics he successfully promoted himself as a champion of the patriotic working man against moralizing Liberal pacifists and do-gooders. Clementine Churchill regarded him as something of a 'rake'.
Oxfordshire Yeomanry Trust

in custody. Only the indignant protests of Lloyd George and Bonar Law prevented further indignities from being heaped upon 'FE' who, as Attorney General, was the ultimate court of appeal for court-marshal cases – and, as such, the superior of the small-minded martinets who were trying to discipline him!

Winston & 'The Other Club'

Winston and F. E. Smith, who had both been blackballed for membership of a political dining club known simply as the 'Club', founded the appropriately-named 'The Other Club' as a retaliatory measure. Its members met fortnightly on Thursdays, when the House of Commons was sitting, in the Pinafore Room at the Savoy Hotel, London. Winston was, in effect, the Chairman and he normally sat in the middle of the table with his back to the Thames. Members included peers, Members of Parliament, military chiefs, press barons and authors. The Other Club had twelve rules – Rule No. 12 being that 'Nothing in the rules or intercourse of the Club shall interfere with the rancour or asperity of party politics'. If thirteen members attended, a large toy black cat was placed next to the Chairman.

Winston was so devoted to The Other Club that he insisted on attending its fortnightly dinners even at the height of The London Blitz. Members of the Other Club included, at various times, Lloyd George, Herbert Kitchener, Admiral Jellicoe, Brendan Brachen, John Lavery, Lawrence Olivier, Robert Menzies, Jan Smuts, Roy Jenkins, Lord Gort, Lord Camrose, Lord Beaverbrook, Lord Rothermere, Arnold Bennett, Lord Gort, Field Marshall Alanbrooke, Edwin Lutyens, Aristotle Onassis and H. G. Wells.

Winston the Gambler

Winston is not generally remembered as a gambler but he was surrounded by a 'racy' set and, not surprisingly, the annual Yeomanry camps were often accompanied by heavy gambling and drinking in the long summer evenings – the principal gamblers being Winston, F. E. Smith, The Earl of Sunderland (known as 'Sunny'), Neil Primrose (Lord Rosebery's son) and Fred Cripps (Stafford's brother). They tried, largely without success, to keep their gambling losses from their wives, who described them as 'the Regency Rakes'.

Winston and his friends also gambled extensively at casinos on the French Riviera and at Monte Carlo, while much gambling took place aboard the Admiralty yacht *Enchantress*. Clementine naturally did not approve, although she was occasionally known to play at the tables for small stakes. At roulette Churchill nearly always played red, while at bridge he was said to be rash, impatient and liable to make every kind of mistake.

Winston's Uniforms

Winston, a natural showman, was the most visible of prime ministers, and although only 5ft 6½ins in height, he was instantly recognizable as he strode through the blitzed areas of London or other cities with a bulldog expression and his famous cigars – the latter being largely 'props' which he would light and flourish but seldom smoke. Hats and uniforms were also part of his distinctive World War II image and, in addition to his normal Westminster attire of bow-tie and striped suit, he also appeared at various times in the uniforms of an air commodore, an elder brother of Trinity House and a colonel of the Queens Own Oxfordshire Hussars. Early in the war he gave up wearing a dinner jacket in favour of a zip-up 'siren suit' which he sometimes wore in public.

Winston, Edward & Mrs Simpson

Winston became friendly with the Prince of Wales during the 1920s, and he clearly hoped that the charismatic young Prince would become a popular and successful monarch. The Prince, who became King Edward VIII in 1936, had a social conscience, and in his short reign he displayed an active interest in the plight of the unemployed. For example, the effects of the Great Depression had been severely felt in many parts of the Welsh coal mining area and, keen to see the effects of the depression at first hand, the uncrowned King carried out a morale-boosting tour of South Wales. This was a source of great concern for Prime Minister Stanley Baldwin, who distrusted the young King's progressive views and had no intention of doing anything to alleviate unemployment.

Unfortunately, Edward had fallen in love with Mrs Wallace Simpson, an American lady, who had divorced two husbands. For this reason she was regarded as an unsuitable consort for a monarch who would also be the Supreme Head of the Church of England.

The Prime Minister, the Anglican establishment and the ruling Conservative Party were all openly hostile towards Edward and Mrs Simpson, and Baldwin seems to have decided that the King would have to abdicate. Winston, a staunch ally of the King, tried everything in his power to prevent an abdication – the idea of a morganatic marriage, whereby Mrs Simpson would have remained a private citizen, being suggested as a compromise solution. Meanwhile, Edward continued to undertake his official duties, including his controversial tour of the designated 'South Wales Special Area'. Sadly, just a few weeks later, Stanley Baldwin brought the constitutional crisis to its inevitable conclusion, and on 10th December the Prime Minister announced the King's abdication. It was, declared Winston, deeply upset, 'the acme of tragedy'.

Winston the Artist

Winston's hobby of painting began, almost by accident, when he picked up a box of watercolour paint boxes belonging to one of his children and made a few tentative brush strokes. He was so pleased with the results that, on the very next day, he ordered an easel, canvases, paints and brushes. His earliest efforts are said to have been interrupted by the arrival of Lady Hazel Lavery (1880-1935), society hostess and beautiful wife of the well-known Irish painter Sir John Lavery (1856-1941). She promptly took command, and taught him to use bold brush-strokes and decisive slashes of paint on the canvas. Sir John Lavery remarked that Winston 'would have made a great master of the brush'. In his book *Thoughts and Adventures* Churchill described the magic moment when he realized he had some artistic talent – it was as though the Muse of Painting had come to his rescue.

Winston's 'Black Dog'

Winston was an emotional individual who suffered throughout his life from periodic bouts of black depression, which he called his 'black dog' days. Although he evidently believed that some hidden hand had protected him from danger at moments of particular crisis, he had no deep religious beliefs to sustain him in his declining years.

As Winston became an old man his mental and physical faculties decayed, and he began to lose the battle that he had fought for so long against the 'black dog' of depression. He found at least some consolation in the warmth and bright colours of the Mediterranean, and he began spending long holidays on the French Riviera. He also enjoyed eight leisurely cruises aboard the 325 ft motor yacht *Christina* as the guest of the Greek shipping magnate Aristotle Onassis (1906-1975) – cruises which must have brought back happy memories of his trips on the steam yacht *Enchantress*, many years before. On one occasion, however, the *Christina* had to pass through the Dardanelles, and the crew were given strict instructions that the passage should be made during the night, so that Winston would not be troubled by unhappy memories of the Gallipoli disaster.

A striking oil-on-board portrait by J. E. Barling depicting Winston Churchill as wartime Prime Minister against an apocalyptic background of storm clouds – note the 'V' discernible in the top right-hand corner of the painting. *Hugh Bourn Collection*

OPERATION 'HOPE NOT'

In April 1963, following a suggestion made by President John F. Kennedy, the United States Congress decided that Sir Winston would be made an Honorary Citizen of the United States – an extremely rare honour that had been granted on only one previous occasion.

On 30th November 1964 Sir Winston celebrated his 90th birthday, and was photographed at the window of his London home, 28 Hyde Park Gate. In the following month he dined for the last time in his London Club. The great statesman was now becoming increasingly frail, and on 15th January 1965 he suffered a stroke, from which he never recovered. Sir Winston Churchill died on Sunday 24th January – seventy years to the day after the death of his father, Lord Randolph Churchill. It was decided that Sir Winston would be given a full state funeral – the last great commoner to have been honoured in this way was The Duke of Wellington, in 1852.

Operation 'Hope Not'

Elaborate preparations for Winston's funeral had already been made, as the former Prime Minister had prepared detailed instructions prior to his death. When the sad news reached Oxfordshire on 24th January, 'Q' Battery of the Queens Own Oxfordshire Hussars were on weekend duty at Banbury. After the news had been received, a moment of silence was observed and the men were then sent home with a warning that they might be called back to take part in the state funeral - possibly to line part of the funeral route as they had during the funeral of Queen Mary, their previous Honorary Colonel, in 1953. It therefore came as something of a surprise when the Battery Commander, Major Timothy L. May, opened the sealed orders marked 'Operation Hope Not' and learned that a detachment of the regiment had been selected, not to guard the route of the funeral but to march in it.

A contingent of three officers and twenty-one other ranks was selected and a drill sergeant from a Guards regiment was brought in to train them in the Drill Hall on Marston Road, Oxford, and on the nearby streets. In addition to practising the slow march step for the funeral, they were taught how to march and rest with arms reversed – a procedure that would not normally have been carried out by Yeomanry gunners.

Two days before the funeral, the Oxfordshire Yeomanry detachment was moved to the Regent's Park Barracks in London so that they could take part in a rehearsal march through the streets of London. For those taking part in the proceedings, this was in many ways a more moving and atmospheric occasion than the funeral itself, as the dress rehearsal took place in the early hours of the morning through the darkened, echoing streets of London - with no sound other that the measured tread of marching feet and the mournful beat of a single drum.

The tension and solemnity of the day itself was lightened by a mildly humorous incident which was entirely in keeping with the independent traditions of the Oxfordshire Yeomanry. According to the instructions, the Queens Own Oxfordshire Hussars were the fifth detachment of soldiers in the procession, which was in effect a place of honour ahead of the coffin and ahead of all the more prestigious Guards regiments. The prominent role allocated to the Oxfordshire Yeomanry during the funeral was most unusual, and one which may have aroused a certain amount of mild jealousy among the Guards officers, who felt that the honour of preceding the coffin should have been theirs. As the procession was forming up, leaving sufficient space for the gun carriage bearing the coffin, a senior Guards officer suggested to Major May that his men were arranged 'incorrectly' according to state funeral protocol. He was completely deflated when the Major replied: 'In the Oxfordshire Yeomanry we always do state funerals this way'. This was a remark worthy of Churchill himself, and one feels that, if Winston was looking down on proceedings, he would have been both pleased and amused!

State Funeral in St. Paul's Cathedral

For three days and three nights 321,000 people silently passed the catafalque in Westminster Hall to pay their last respects to the great commoner, while on Saturday 30th January 1965 the funeral cortege left for St Paul's Cathedral. The coffin was carried on a gun carriage and draped with a large Union flag, and on top was a black cushion supporting the insignia of the Order of the Garter.

The procession was led by Clementine in the Queen's town coach, and Winston's son Randolph followed the gun-carriage on foot. All three services were represented, and in addition to a Royal Naval escort, a contingent of Guards and the Queens Own Oxfordshire Hussars, a

Members of The Queens Own Oxfordshire Hussars funeral party. *Oxfordshire Yeomanry Trust OXFYT409*

Bugle & Sabre Special

The iconic image of Winston Churchill as the leader of his country during World War II. From a print by the Hungarian-born artist Arthur Pan.
Hugh Bourn Collection

"Not merely does Churchill bestride the century, not merely has he been the foremost performer in British and world politics for a longer period than almost any rival in ancient or modern times. The same giant lineaments are revealed when his particular faculties are examined. His vitality, his brainpower, his endurance, his wit, his eloquence, his industry, his application were superabundant, superhuman …. The man was huge"
Michael Foot

Right: Winston in bronze, by Simon Manby, specially commissioned by Hugh Bourn.
Hugh Bourn Collection

In 1922 Winston purchased the run-down Chartwell Manor, in Kent, and having carried out an extensive renovation, he moved in to his new home in 1924. Thereafter, Chartwell became both his home and his political headquarters.

The National Portrait Gallery

Winston's monumental four-volume history of his ancestor, the first Duke of Marlborough.

Hugh Bourn Collection

Winston's Publications

The Story of the Malakand Field Force (1898)
The River War (1899)
Savrola (1900)
London to Ladysmith via Pretoria (1900)
Ian Hamilton's March (1900)
Lord Randolph Churchill (1906)
My African Journey (1908)
Liberalism and the Social Problem (1910)
The World Crisis (4 volumes 1923-29)
My Early Life (1930)
The Eastern Front (1931)
Thoughts and Adventures (1932)
Marlborough (4 volumes 1933-38)
Great Contemporaries (1937)
Arms and the Covenant (speeches 1938)
Step by Step (1939)
Into Battle (speeches 1941)
The Unrelenting Struggle (speeches 1942)
The End of the Beginning (speeches 1943)
Onwards to Victory (speeches 1944)
The Dawn of Liberation (speeches 1945)
Victory (1946)
Secret Session (speeches 1946)
The Sinews of Peace (speeches 1948)
Painting as a Pastime (1948)
Europe Unite (speeches 1950)
In the Balance (speeches 1951)
Stemming the Tide (speeches 1951-53)
The Unwritten Alliance
    (speeches 1953-59 1961)

The Second World War

Vol. 1 *The Gathering Storm* (1948)
Vol. 2 *Their Finest Hour* (1949)
Vol. 3 *The Grand Alliance* (1950)
Vol. 4 *The Hinge of Fate* (1951)
Vol. 5 *Closing the Ring* (1952)
Vol. 6 *Triumph and Tragedy* (1954)

A History of the English-Speaking Peoples

Vol. 1 *The Birth of Britain* (1956)
Vol. 2 *The New World* (1956)
Vol. 3 *The Age of Revolution* (1957)
Vol. 4 *The Great Democracies* (1958)

Royal Air Force band played Handel's Death March. Big Ben chimed ten o'clock and was silent for the rest of the day. In St. James's Park, the first of ninety guns began their salute – one for each year of his life.

In St. Paul's Cathedral, the hushed congregation of 3,500 people included the Queen, five other monarchs, five heads of state and sixteen prime ministers. General Eisenhower, General Charles de Gaulle and Marshal Komev were present, while other mourners included Anthony Eden, Harold Macmillan, Lord Mountbatten, Clement Attlee and Robert Menzies. The hymns included Winston's favourites – *The Battle Hymn of the American Republic*, *Fight the Good Fight* and *Oh God, Our Help in Ages Past*.

The Dockers' Salute

At the conclusion of the service the coffin was taken to the Tower of London Pier and piped aboard the Port of London Authority motor launch *Havengore*, after which a flotilla of launches carried the family upstream to Waterloo, accompanied by the strains of *Rule Britannia* and the sound of a 19-gun salute from the Hon Artillery Company guns at the Tower. Sixteen RAF Lightning fighters swept overhead as the coffin was conveyed up the Thames, but the most memorable and strangely moving gesture of mourning during this part of the journey was provided by the London dockers, who saluted the dead statesman in unique fashion by lowering the jibs of their cranes as the flotilla swept past.

The Final Rail Journey to Bladon

Sir Winston's body was then conveyed from Waterloo to Handborough station by special train, the 78-mile route being via Clapham Junction, Richmond, Staines and Ascot to Reading, where the special gained access to the Great Western main line for the final part of the journey through Didcot and Oxford. The train was hauled, appropriately enough, by the 135-ton 'Battle of Britain' class locomotive No. 34051 *Winston Churchill*, while the formation included Pullman parlour brake No. 208, special hearse van No. S2464, and the Pullman cars *Carina*, *Lydia*, *Perseus* and *Isle of Thanet*.

Silent crowds lined the route of the funeral train, while the sombre nature of the weather reflected the poignancy of the occasion. At Wolvercot Junction the special swung north-westwards onto the Oxford, Worcester & Wolverhampton line and, within a few minutes, it had reached its destination at Handborough, where the ancient wooden station building was draped in purple crepe to disguise its ramshackle appearance. From Handborough, Winston's body was taken by hearse for a private burial in St. Martin's churchyard at Bladon, near Woodstock – his final resting place being beside the graves of Lord and Lady Randolph Churchill, and within site of his birthplace at neighbouring Blenheim Palace.

The Queens Own Oxfordshire Hussars funeral party in training for their role in the Winston's funeral procession.
Oxfordshire Yeomanry Trust OXYT409